6 6^{95}

79-354 ✓

HV5740
.R67   Ross, Walter S.

        You can quit smoking in
        14 days.

You Can
Quit Smoking
in 14 Days

You Can Quit Smoking in 14 Days

by Walter S. Ross

Reader's Digest Press
Distributed by E. P. Dutton & Co., Inc.
New York 1974

Library of Congress Cataloging in Publication Data

Ross, Walter Sanford
You can quit smoking in 14 days.

1. Cigarette habit.   2. Smoking.   I. Title
HV5740.R67   613.8'5   74-7344
ISBN 0-88349-033-1

Published simultaneously in Canada by Clarke, Irwin & Company
Limited, Toronto and Vancouver

Portions of this material have appeared in *Reader's Digest* in slightly
different form.

To the 45 million Americans
who would like to stop smoking;
and to the 29 million who
have done so

CONTENTS

DIRECTIONS

It will be necessary to leave
off Tobacco. But I had some thoughts
of doing that before, for I sometimes
think it does not agree with me.

Charles Lamb
Letter to Wordsworth

This book was written to help the great majority of American smokers—45 million of the present 52 million smoking population—who, surveys tell us, would like to quit smoking.

It is organized into 14 Days. Eleven of these are Action Days in which you do something to give you insight into your smoking and to help you quit. Three Days are for Reading; these give you important background information and a number of practical tips on Actions that you may take later.

You can read this book in a sitting. But we recommend that you don't. Follow the Days—Day by Day—to give yourself time to assimilate much new information and many fresh insights into yourself and your habit—and to let the book work for you.

Quitting cigarettes isn't an *act,* it's a *process.* In most people who stop smoking the process has gone on subconsciously, often for a couple of years, before being transformed into a new habit pattern. It's possible to speed the procedure, and to make it more effective, by dividing it into steps and organizing these in a progressive sequence. Scientists call such an activity a learning experience.

You can teach yourself not to smoke, just as you taught yourself to smoke. That too was a learning experience.

Quitting is triggered by something that makes you think about it. This happens quite frequently to most smokers. The reaction is fortified and transformed into a motivation for quitting by what you want out of life—your values, your goals—and how they relate to smoking (See Day Seven).

But there is a long step between motivation and action. The gap has to be bridged by understanding. You must learn why you started to smoke (Day One, Section 4), what smoking has come to mean to you (Day Two), and how it is reinforced or impeded by the world around you (Day Ten).

On Day Eleven you begin to put your new knowledge and insights together, and on Day Thirteen you will probably be ready to try out your new habit pattern that does not include smoking.

Two weeks is an arbitrary, but reasonable, time span to relearn the habit you had before you became a smoker. Remember, it took months for you to learn to smoke and enjoy it. It took many years for smoking to braid itself into the pattern of your life—to be involved with your leisure, your pleasure, your pain, your triumphs, and your defeats; your meals, your digestion, your coffee breaks, your cocktail hours; your love making, your fears, your exhilarations, your depressions, your waking, your sleeping, your work, and your play. To detach a habit so long cherished and so deeply enmeshed with your personality and your life takes time, care, and understanding.

INTRODUCTION

Tobacco hic,
If a man be well it will make him sick.

> John Ray
> *English Proverbs*

There's no law that says you have to give up cigarettes. If they didn't provide pleasure and a variety of satisfactions, 52 million Americans wouldn't be inhaling their smoke.

And if science hadn't discovered during the past ten or fifteen years that what was once thought to be merely a bad habit, perhaps harmful to children but not to adults, actually poses serious, even lethal, dangers to people of all ages, there would be little reason for quitting.

But now it has been proved beyond any reasonable doubt that smoking is the greatest single cause of human disease, disability, and death in the environment. The British Royal College of Physicians calls it "as important a cause of death as were the great epidemic diseases such as typhoid, cholera, and tuberculosis." And the U.S. Public Health Service describes it as "the foremost cause of preventable disease and death in this country."

It's because so many smokers have been convinced by these authoritative opinions, and the mountain of scientific evidence behind them, that they want to give up their habit. There are other motives, too, as we will see, but health is central to most of them.

The author of this book is, like every other former smoker, an expert on quitting. I smoked one to two packs a day of unfiltered cigarettes, on and off, for about thirty years until I stopped in March 1968. I did not quit for health reasons but because I wasn't enjoying ,smoking enough to warrant accepting the tired feeling, cough, and other unpleasant effects.

I had been researching and writing about this subject for a dozen years for the American Cancer Society and later for *Reader's Digest*. However, I was not really convinced by the health evidence until after I stopped smoking. It wasn't because I was looking for ex post facto reasons to justify my quitting. And neither the *Reader's Digest* nor the American Cancer Society forbid people who work with or for them to smoke. I quit because it suited me, and accepted the evidence when it convinced me. I believe that every smoker should approach the subject the same way. I not only don't believe in exhorting or frightening smokers or doing anything to force them to quit, but actively oppose such methods. However, I have seen at firsthand in many parts of the country a passionate and overwhelming demand by countless smokers for help in quitting. Therefore, it seems reasonable to offer what assistance I can.

W. S. R.

DAY ONE

Earth ne'er did breed
Such a jovial weed.

       Barten Holyday
       Technogamia

This is a Reading Day, in which you study the first four chapters for background—rules for quitting, the role of nicotine, the connection between emotions and the smoking habit, the reasons why you started to smoke, and the way to quit.

1. "Please Don't Stop Smoking"
Ten Rules for Quitting

Tobacco is . . . rather taken of many for wantonnes
when they have nothing else to do
than of any absolute or necessary use.

Edmund Gardiner
The Trial of Tobacco

How is quitting cigarettes like ending a love affair?
"At first you think you can't live without your lover. But
then you meet someone new, and life begins again. That's
the way it is with cigarettes; after a while, you'll begin to
think of them as an old flame."

This riddle is from an American Cancer Society manual
that helps people to quit smoking cigarettes. The manual is
part of the new wave of research-based help that is aiding
thousands of people to kick their habit.

The new information and techniques are the result of an
enormous demand created by a powerful shift in smokers'
attitudes and actions in recent years. In 1966 a survey of a
random cross section of smokers showed that 56 percent of
the adult United States smoking population had thought
seriously about stopping and about 36 percent had tried.

But only 7 percent had been able to give up cigarettes. About half these smokers were reinterviewed in 1970. There had been a dramatic change. By then, fully 87 percent of the men and 84 percent of the women said they had thought seriously about giving up cigarettes—an enormous 50 percent jump in would-be quitters in about four years. The proportion of those who had tried to quit had risen to 60 percent; the net stopping rate for men was up to 26 percent and for women to 21 percent. In other words, nearly four times as many men and three times as many women were quitting as in 1966. The coughing minority—smokers represent only about 36 percent of the adult population— was getting smaller.

There is a normal smoking attrition among smokers in their fifties and sixties. About two million quit every year because smoking has become painful or unpleasant. Many are warned by their doctors to stop. They have often developed symptoms of a smoking-related disease that reinforce the doctor's warning. For most of these people quitting is comparatively easy.

Today, this normal population of quitters has been augmented by many millions. In 1964 a government survey revealed about 17 million ex-smokers in the U.S. population. In 1966, two years after the first Surgeon General's report, this number had gone up to only 19 million. But in the next four years—1966–1970—the figure rose sharply and dramatically to 29 million who had made the switch to clean air.

Smokers have never been in the majority. In 1966 about half the men and less than a third of the women in the United States smoked tobacco. In 1970 the percentages had dropped in both groups: to about 40 percent of men and 31 percent of women.

If trends had continued as they were before the health scare began affecting cigarette sales in the late fifties and early sixties, there would be today about 75 million smokers in this country. But there are only 52 million.* Today, 23.5 percent of U.S. adults are ex-smokers. To help the millions who would like to join them, an enormous variety of methods and techniques have been developed: these include highly organized medical programs given by hospitals, classes, fear-arousing lectures and literature, programed learning, role playing, positive thinking, books, movies, nicotine substitutes, medications in the form of pills, lozenges, chewing gum, injections, mouthwashes and other drugstore remedies, mail-order techniques, sensory deprivation (staying in a dark, sound-proof room), sleep records, exercises, social pressure, bets, five-day plans, stimulus satiation, aversion techniques and conditioning (making smoking repellent), personal counseling from physicians, ministers, social workers, health educators and others, discussion groups, and psychoanalysis.

There are groups like SmokEnders and Smoke-Watchers, who offer group therapy at reasonable fees with a frank profit motive, which is not a condemnation. Paying money for help in quitting may actually aid some people to make the necessary commitment. There is the Schick method (developed by the razor people) which offers individual counseling plus electroshock aversion therapy at a cost of several hundred dollars. The Seventh Day Adventists, a religious group that forbids its members to smoke, runs nonsectarian, intensive, five-day groups which insist that anyone who enters must stop smoking from the start. (One has been run in a Long Island railroad commuter car.) Some pyschiatrists and psychologists offer individual counseling, with or without hypnotism, for substantial fees. The

---

* Most people believe that a majority of the adult population smokes. But the cigarette companies know better—and saw the trends. More than ten years ago they began diversifying, buying up dog food, liquor, and other companies, and even changing their names. American Tobacco is now American Brands, as one example.

American Cancer Society has worked out a group method something like Alcoholics Anonymous and Weight Watchers with no fees, which can be done without professional help (see Day Eleven, Section 3).

Most of these programs have some degree of success because almost anything will work if a smoker wants to quit badly enough. In fact, if he is sufficiently strongly motivated, he can quit by himself without any guidance or help. Unfortunately, only about 5 percent of smokers are in this category at any one time.

The president of a professional stop-smoking program says that the barriers that block people from even considering giving up smoking are fears; first, the fear of stopping, because smokers may have tried stopping without proper preparation, and found it somewhat painful. Second, they fear failure, and this, too, is based on their own experience and perhaps that of their friends. Their third fear is of being unable to function without cigarettes.

All of these fears are based on reality. But each can be overcome.

Most people who want to quit need nothing more than you will find in these pages. Says Dr. Donald T. Fredrickson, "Every smoker can conquer the cigarette habit irrespective of how addicted, how defeated, or discouraged he may feel, or how many times he has temporarily stopped. Only a small percentage of smokers require professional support to be successful in quitting." Dr. Fredrickson knows whereof he speaks, for he has devoted much of his professional life to devising ways to help smokers quit and helping them to do so.

What this book provides is the distilled experience, information, and techniques, in self-help form, that have worked for thousands of ex-smokers in all parts of the country—everybody from four-cigarette-a-day tenderthroats as young as twelve years of age to four-pack-a-day chain smokers in their seventies.

To sum up: *Ten Rules for Quitting Cigarettes*

Rule 1. The first thing to know is that *it doesn't take will power to quit cigarettes.* "I don't know what will power is," says David Witti, a young California behavior therapist. "We never discuss will power with smokers. What we talk about is motivation." Witti works with teen-age delinquents, to whom smoking is only slightly less natural than breathing. The fact that you have read this far probably indicates that you are seriously thinking about stopping smoking: you are motivated. That gives you an edge. But your motivation has to be strong enough to produce and support action. By reading on, you are taking the first step toward that action.

Rule 2. The basic concept of our method of quitting is that *smoking is a learning experience*—an experience you can unlearn. Remember, *you weren't born a smoker.* At first you probably got sick. It took weeks, maybe even months, before you weren't a little dizzy from the first smoke of the day. And even today, if you smoke too much doesn't it sometimes give you a headache or an upset stomach?

Rule 3. *It took years to develop your smoking habit.* You can't root out something that deep overnight. If you're like 95 percent of smokers, you shouldn't even try, because you probably won't be able to do it that quickly. If it proves impossible, as it well may, you'll feel a failure. This is a normal pattern in smokers—it is what keeps so many smoking. They just know they can't quit, because they've tried.

Rule 4. So, rather than urge you to try to stop smoking, we advise you: *Please don't try to quit smoking,* not before you've learned why you smoke and your motives for quitting.

Rule 5. Most people who have stopped smoking will say that they quit "cold turkey." But actually, research shows that many went through an unrealized cutting-down process for years. Perhaps a few years ago they dropped from two packs a day to a pack and a half, then later to a pack, and then to fifteen or ten cigarettes. They'd been weaning themselves without realizing it.

You can do this consciously by our method in a much shorter time. But again, please don't try any action yet—you're probably not ready to cut down. *Continue to smoke your regular dose while you continue to read.*

Rule 6. *Don't judge yourself.* Don't set up any kind of preconceived schedule or goal. Don't compare yourself with others who have tried and succeeded—or failed.

Rule 7. *Quitting isn't easy,* even for those who have been able to do it. Anyone who tells you that it's a cinch to kick the habit either has never smoked or has no insight into your problem.

Rule 8. But *quitting need not be all that difficult or painful,* either. How else were so many millions of smokers—some of whom did away with upward of eighty cigarettes (four packs) a day—able to kick the habit?

Rule 9. *There's no magic button* that will suddenly turn you off tobacco. There is no drug, potion, or incantation guaranteed to work all of the time or all of a sudden. But there is no mystery to quitting. You can do it a lot more easily if you understand the process and follow it step by step to suit your own wishes and needs.

Rule 10. *Smoking is intensely personal.* You had your own reasons for starting, your own motives for continuing. And you should make your own decisions about quitting, in your own good time. Don't let anyone rush you.

2. Why Do People Smoke? Nicotine

Divine in hookas, glorious in a pipe
When tipp'd with amber, mellow, rich, and ripe;
Like other charmers, wooing the caress
More dazzlingly when daring in full dress;
Yet thy true lovers more admire by far
Thy naked beauties—give me a cigar!

> George Noel Gordon, Lord Byron
> *The Island II*

Endemic in the human condition seems to be the need to escape it. In 1846 Dr. Thomas Laycock wrote, "There appears to be an instinctive craving in man for things which act on the nervous system." Later scientists have noted that chemicals which change minds and moods have an attraction for the human race that is close to a basic drive, like hunger and sex. The craving is sometimes so strong that at different times and places people, to get their fix, have accepted such side effects as hallucinations and paralysis, malnutrition, violent vomiting and convulsions, the destruction of vital organs, and even death.

Because the craving persists, and the means for satisfying it are only temporary, the mood-changing or mind-bending drug must be retaken. In almost all cases tolerance develops, necessitating larger and more frequent doses. The taking of the drug becomes as important as the effect; it reinforces itself and becames an end in itself—a habit, a dependency, or an addiction.

In general, most of the habit-forming substances craved by large groups of people for a long time have come from plants. These substances include such relatively innocuous chemicals as caffeine in tea, coffee, and cocoa; arecoline in betel nuts, and such powerful drugs as cannabinols in marijuana, pseudoephedrine (khat), cocaine from cocoa leaves, and morphine and heroin from opium.

Tobacco belongs in this group, somewhere between coffee and betel nut. Like these plants it has an active, habituating ingredient, nicotine—a poison, found in nature only in tobacco.

Nobody has ever proved it, but just about every scientist who has looked into the problem assumes that nicotine is the psychotropic drug that makes using tobacco a habit.

Experiments with smokers indicate that there is an optimal dose of nicotine for each user—they'll reject too much and want more if they get too little. Giving smokers injections of nicotine slightly reduced the number of cigarettes they smoked; giving them nicotine capsules orally had a similar but lesser effect. That was when the smokers were allowed to use their regular brands. But when they were given brands with filters of different nicotine-removal efficiency, smokers of the high-retention filter cigarettes took more frequent puffs and managed to obtain about the same amount of nicotine as those who smoked the low-efficiency filters. "The results support the notion that smokers automatically adjust the nicotine dose from cigarettes to an 'optimal' level," says Dr. Edwin F. Domino of the University of Michigan.

This is consistent with experiments in which laboratory animals are permitted to select their own dosage of various reinforcing drugs such as alcohol, amphetamines, barbiturates, cocaine, and morphine. Left to themselves, the animals will take only that quantity of the given drug that gives them the effect they seek, adjusting frequency of intake to the size of the dose.

Why do people crave nicotine? "There is growing evidence that nicotine, and/or possibly an integral part of the smoking act, exerts a tranquilizing action on the central nervous system," says Dr. Barbara B. Brown of the Veterans Administration Hospital in Sepulveda, California. Dr. Brown has proved that smokers have brain wave patterns different from nonsmokers, which may account for their desire for nicotine. After three cigarettes, a smoker's slow brain waves show distinct electroencephalographic changes.

Like several other habituating drugs—amphetamine, cocaine, and caffeine—nicotine acts on those nerves in the body that release a substance known as acetylcholine, which affects the heart, the blood vessels, the gastrointestinal system, and other organs controlled by the sympathetic nerves.

But unlike the strongly addictive drugs, nicotine is self-limiting: if you take too much, you get nicotine poisoning. Smokers do acquire a small amount of tolerance to tobacco, but this is totally unlike the tolerance that users of the addictive drugs build up, which forces them to take larger and larger doses to achieve their high.

Tobacco tolerance takes two forms. One is low-grade tolerance to the smoke, in the mucous membranes of the mouth, throat, and lungs. This kind of tolerance occurs whenever living tissues are repeatedly exposed to local irritants, for they become less sensitive to the irritants.

The second form of tobacco tolerance is to nicotine itself. Smokers are able to take somewhat larger doses of this alkaloid than are nonsmokers, but as noted this tolerance is small and limited.

The third form of tolerance might better be called toleration. Smokers become so habituated to smoke that they will put up with symptoms of tissue irritation and nicotine poisoning which are unacceptable to the novice smoker. Heavy smokers live with their chronic coughing and spitting as necessary evils. Some become accustomed to recurrent attacks of nausea and most to a rapid heartbeat.

If cigarettes contain a mind- or mood-changing substance, does this mean that cigarette smokers are addicts, like heroin addicts? The only honest answer is that there is no clear-cut line between addiction and habituation. The World Health Organization Expert Committee on Drugs Liable to Produce Addiction attempted to separate the two as follows:

DRUG ADDICTION	DRUG HABITUATION
Drug addiction is a state of periodic or chronic intoxication produced by the repeated consumption of a drug (natural or synthetic). Its characteristics include:	Drug habituation (habit) is a condition resulting from the repeated consumption of a drug. Its characteristics include:
1) An overpowering desire or need (compulsion) to continue taking the drug and to obtain it by any means;	1) A desire (but not compulsion) to continue taking the drug for the sense of improved well-being which it engenders;
2) A tendency to increase the dose;	2) Little or no tendency to increase the dose;
3) A psychic (psychological) and generally a physical dependence on the effects of the drug;	3) Some degree of psychic dependence on the effect of the drug, but absence of physical dependence and hence of an abstinence syndrome;
4) Detrimental effects on the individual and on society.	4) Detrimental effects, if any, primarily on the individual.

You can fit tobacco partially into either of these definitions, depending on the smoker. There are people who need cigarettes so badly that they will do nearly anything to get them, although, unlike the heroin addict, they are unlikely to kill for a smoke.

There was the woman whose doctor warned her that on-rushing emphysema would reduce her to invalidism if she didn't stop smoking. She shut herself on a New England mountaintop, without a car, far from the nearest tobacco-nist, with an ample supply of tranquilizers and booze. In ten days she was down on the road scrounging for stray butts discarded by passing motorists.

A man who lost his larynx to cancer brought on by heavy smoking devised a kind of cigarette holder that fit into the breathing hole the surgeons left in his neck. He continued to inhale smoke directly into his lungs with this device.

Are such people addicts, or merely strongly habituated? Does it matter?

Most of the ex-drug addicts at Synanon, the famous drug rehabilitation center in California, have become heavy cig-arette smokers. They claim that cigarettes are harder to kick than heroin. But it's known that hard-drug addicts usually suffer from psychologic or psychiatric disorders which show themselves in other ways if the drugs are removed. Drug taking, in other words, is only a symptom.

A Canadian doctor has attempted to draw a parallel be-tween the history of opium and that of tobacco. For seven thousand years opium was smoked in pipes, and it wasn't an overwhelming problem. Opium smokers were like Saturday night drunks; once a week was enough. But when science began extracting the active ingredients such as morphine and heroin from opium, and the hypodermic needle per-mitted direct injection, then the Saturday night habit be-came an irresistible addiction.

This physician, Dr. R. Denson of Saskatoon, Saskatche-wan, finds a parallel in the change in smoking habits and the rise of addictive smokers. The American Indians, the first users of tobacco, smoked it sparingly in pipes, and so did the early European smokers. The cigar, snuff, and chewing tobacco were other forms. Then came the cigarette,* which was brought to Europe by British soldiers who served in the Crimean War. Made of heat-cured tobaccos, cigarettes give off an acid smoke much easier to inhale than pipe or cigar smoke. In fact, though pipes and cigars release their nicotine to the tissues of the mouth because of their heavy, alkaline smoke, making it unnecessary as well as unpleasant to inhale, cigarettes give up nicotine more reluctantly. The smoker has to inhale the light, acid smoke into his lungs in order to extract enough nicotine for his satisfaction. Because of their tissuelike consistency, the lungs offer the smoke and the nicotine almost direct access to the bloodstream. Inhaling cigarette smoke is, Dr. Denson says, something like mainlining heroin or morphine.

Denson carries the analogy further. He sees a parallel between the withdrawal symptoms of the person attempting to kick the hard-drug habit and the sometimes nervous reactions of some people who give up cigarettes. This parallel seems farfetched. The withdrawal symptoms of heroin and other such drugs are life threatening, but nobody ever came close to dying as the result of quitting cigarettes.

Smoking tobacco is closer to betel nut chewing than to other drug habits. Several hundred million people chew betel nut. A more difficult habit to break than cigarette smoking, the custom starts in infancy and continues to death. Like tobacco, betel nut gives off a chemical (arecoline) which is a mild stimulant to the central nervous system. But if you

---

* " 'Cigarette' means: (1) any roll of tobacco wrapped in paper or in any substance not containing tobacco, and (2) any roll of tobacco wrapped in any substance containing tobacco which, because of its appearance, the type of tobacco used in the filler, or its packaging and labeling, is likely to be offered to, or purchased by, consumers as a cigarette described in paragraph (1)." From Title 26—Internal Revenue Code, Subtitle E—Alcohol, Tobacco, and certain other Excise Taxes; Chapter 52—Cigars, Cigarettes, and Cigarette Papers and Tubes (As enacted by P.L. 85-859, effective September 3, 1958, and as amended by P.L. 89-44, effective January 1, 1966).

dose betel nut chewers with straight arecoline without their chaw, most can barely detect it. The same is true of cigarette smokers. Give them cigarettes with less nicotine than their regular brands and only a few will consciously notice the difference. Give them straight nicotine, either orally or by injection, and they will cut down only a little on their smoking. Obviously, then, chewing betel nuts or smoking cigarettes is done for something other than just the chemical reaction.

The best definition of habit we have found is "a fixed behavior pattern overlearned to the point of becoming automatic and marked by decreasing awareness and increasing dependence on secondary, rather than primary, reinforcement." *

This describes smoking perfectly. There is a certain degree of physical dependence on nicotine but little tolerance and no demand for an ever-increasing dose. Giving up this stabilized habit involves no real physical withdrawal symptoms. If there are nervous symptoms, they are usually mild, minimal, and controllable.

The strong habituating element in smoking is those secondary reinforcers that researchers mention—not the nicotine, not the need for it, but the connections that smoking has come to have with so many parts of the smoker's personality and daily life. These, as we will see in the next chapter, are the core of the problem. The only serious physical consequence of giving up smoking is a general improvement in health.

* William A. Hunt and Joseph D. Matarazzo, "Habit Mechanisms in Smoking," in *Learning Mechanisms in Smoking,* ed. Hunt (Chicago: Aldine Publishing Co., 1970).

3. Why Do People Smoke? Emotions

There's nothing like tobacco; it is the pas-
sion of all decent men; a man who lives
without tobacco does not deserve to live.

Molière

"There would be no need to create a committee on tobacco," says Dr. Hans Selye, the world authority on stress
and disease, "if nobody found smoking cigarettes advanta-
geous or desirable." And, says Dr. Daniel Horn, head of the
National Clearinghouse for Smoking and Health, a government agency, "The cigarette caught hold because it fulfills
certain functions that need to be fulfilled for a great many
people."

Smoking, in other words, isn't just a means of satisfying
a craving for nicotine. Smoking is a sensual act, involving
sight, smell, taste, and oral gratification of the sucking reflex, which dates back to everyone's infancy.

And, further, smoking is often associated in the minds of
the young with sophistication and maturity. Also, offering a
cigarette or a light is a social icebreaker, creating a bond

between strangers. Smoking gives the smoker something to do with his hands in public. It is also a ritual which becomes associated with different situations in life—both good and bad. "A cigarette offers an accessible, inexpensive way of dealing with a variety of problems," says Dr. Horn.

As the Advisory Committee to the Surgeon General says, "The overwhelming evidence points to the conclusion that smoking—its beginning, habituation, and occasional discontinuation—is to a large extent psychologically and socially determined. This does not rule out physiological factors, especially in respect to habituation, nor the existence of predisposing constitutional or hereditary factors."

Until a few years ago, there was very little help for the smoker who wanted to quit. And what help there was was based on trial and error—many trials, lots of errors.

But today, "smoking cessation," as the experts call it, is now much better understood, better organized, and more effective. Most of the key systems that actually help people to quit smoking and stay off cigarettes are based on the psychological principles of a researcher in that field, Silvan S. Tomkins, Ph.D.

Dr. Tomkins started with the assumption that smoking is oral behavior. Psychological experiments prove that though there is a biological drive for mouth activity necessary to satisfy hunger, there is also a drive for mouth activity *independent* of the hunger drive. This was confirmed by a series of experiments in which puppies were fed from bottles with large-holed nipples and small-holed nipples. Those that took their milk from the large-holed nipples got their food rather quickly but then continued to suck on the experimenter's finger, or on each other, afterward, while the group that sucked on the small-holed nipples had to suck harder and longer to get the same amount of food. The longer and harder sucking seemed to satisfy their need for this kind of activity, and they were less likely to suck on the researcher's finger after their hunger had been satisfied.

This sucking drive can develop into a habit independent of food when it becomes linked with emotional situations, as in the thumb sucking of a child. There is a relationship here with the smoking habit. What starts in part as oral gratification becomes linked with a whole range of activities and emotions. "The key to the understanding of smoking behavior is to be found in the management of affect," says Dr. Tomkins. ("Affect" is a technical term for human feelings or emotions.)

There are eight primary emotions. Three—excitement, enjoyment, and surprise—are positive, while five—distress, anger, fear, shame, and contempt—are negative. Linked with these basic emotions are two forms of behavior: smiling, which goes with positive affects, and crying (real or symbolic, as frowning), associated with the negative emotions.

People are programed from birth to get the most out of their positive feelings (to smile), and to minimize their unpleasant emotions (to stop crying). And from birth they find that sucking—and, later, smoking—can do both of these things. "So," says Tomkins, "we may learn to pick up a cigarette to make us feel less afraid, less angry, less ashamed, less disgusted. We may also learn to pick up a cigarette to give us a positive affective lift of excitement."

Paul Nesbitt, while a Ph.D. candidate at Columbia University, spotted a basic paradox in smokers. There is ample evidence that the physiological effects of smoking are those of arousal and stimulation—a faster heartbeat, a rise in blood pressure. Yet the great majority of smokers, when questioned as to what they get out of smoking cigarettes, will say something like "it relaxes me" or "it calms me."

Thus, a known stimulant is described by many users to be a tranquilizer. Why is this? Part of the explanation may be a physical dependence on nicotine. The smoker craves his fix and, when it arrives in the smoke of his cigarette, he feels gratified and satisfied. The effect, therefore, seems relaxing or calming.

To explain how smoking, which is never pleasant at first and can often be actually nauseating, can become a habit, experts in smoking withdrawal have adopted the learning theory of B. F. Skinner, the behavioral psychologist. The fact that understanding this theory helps many more people to stop smoking than did older methods (which relied on scaring and/or "educating" the smoker) indicates that the experts are on the right track.

According to Skinner, behavior is learned because it is linked up with something that happens immediately afterward to reinforce it—a "positive reinforcer" is the technical term. If the behavior is followed by a "negative reinforcer" (punishment or something unpleasant), the behavior is less likely to recur.

So, for example, when a child begins to try out cigarettes, he doesn't like them and may even hate them, but he usually smokes them with others who applaud him and tell him how good cigarettes are. After a while he doesn't need these social reinforcers. He comes to like cigarettes because he has linked them with positive emotions. If a man smokes a cigarette every time he takes a work break, a relaxing time, then eventually the cigarette comes to represent relaxation.

Positive Reinforcement

Stimulus	Response	Reward	External Reinforcement
Coffee	Smoking	Sophistication	Advertising

To change behavior, there are two possibilities. You can provide a negative reinforcer (which is difficult to do; electric-shock aversion therapy is an attempt at this), or "you can increase the positive, competing behaviors," according to Dr. Richard C. Grant, associate professor of psychiatry at the University of Oregon. Continues Dr. Grant, "You cannot engage in nonsmoking behavior; there is no such thing. . . . You can only do something else instead of smoking. There's no vacuum of behavior, just like you can't stop communicating."

Current successful programs to help people stop smoking concentrate on the conscious replacement of smoking with positive, competing behaviors, thus avoiding the attempt at *non*behavior.

4. Why Did You Start to Smoke— and How Can You Quit?

He who does not smoke hath either known great griefs, or refuseth himself the softest consolation, next to that which comes from Heaven.

> Lord Lytton
> *What Will He Do With It?*

Because almost all Americans who smoke cigarettes began to do so between the ages of twelve and twenty, psychologists and sociologists have made hundreds of studies to find out why they started smoking and why a majority of children of the same ages did not. For the fact is that though a vast majority, about 80 percent or more, of children experiment with smoking, only a small portion actually become regular smokers. And a very large number who do start quit while still teen-agers. In a recent survey, 40 percent of the boys and 24 percent of the girls between twelve and eighteen described themselves as ex-smokers.

What factors are apt to distinguish smoking children from their nonsmoking friends?

A boy is more likely to smoke if both of his parents do. For a girl the important parental influence is her mother.

More recent research indicates that the smoking behavior of children also relates to the way they feel about their parents. If the children are in revolt and their parents smoke, there is a good chance that the children will not take up the habit. And the reverse is true: those children who admire their parents tend to imitate their habits. If the parents smoke, the children will; if not, not. The generally held belief that all children regard smoking as desirable does not seem to be true. It has more to do with the way they feel about their parents and what their parents do.

Smokers tend to come from large families and to have older brothers and sisters who smoke. The influence of their friends is also very powerful. Adolescence is a period when a child is in the process of reducing his dependence on his family and parents and is shifting it to others of his own age. There is a very strong tendency for smoking children to have smoking friends, and the opposite is also true; nonsmokers run together.

A number of studies indicate that smokers feel inadequate in relation to others of their age. Young smokers generally don't have a very high regard for themselves; they seem to be afraid that they can't make it. They also worry and complain more than nonsmokers about their school work, their health, and their world. The fact is that smoking children do have more anxiety and more physical complaints than do nonsmokers. Young smokers see themselves as bored, in search of thrills; they realize that they tend to act out their aggressions in unpopular ways. They are not satisfied to be their age. They want to appear older, so they act the way they think adults act, they smoke and drink, and they experiment with sex more than do nonsmokers.

Smokers are usually poorer students. In one study only 8 percent of A students were smokers, but 60 percent of D students smoked. Cause or effect? Although in very small quantities nicotine does stimulate the brain, heavy smokers tend to be duller in their responses than nonsmokers. Tests prove that young smokers generally do worse in school than they are capable of doing. The childhood smoker tends to be older than his classmates, too. Researchers think that their smoking compensates for not keeping up with their own age group and for poorer grades, and is a way of coping with the anxieties that these create. For most children do worry about their grades. Smoking children arc more apt to drop out of school, and they tend to choose the easier subjects to study.

It is interesting and important that the one quality that smoking children admire in their nonsmoking peers is academic success. Nonsmokers are usually rated by all their classmates, smokers and nonsmokers alike, as being the best all-around kids, the ones most likely to succeed in life. It is also interesting that of children who expect to go to college only one in five is a smoker, a proportion considerably below the average of smokers in their age group.

Only about 3 percent of boys and 2 percent of girls are smoking before age twelve. Some men only begin to smoke when they take their first job or enter military service. There are several possible explanations, but the central one seems to be that when smoking starts in adulthood it is as a response to stress.

Smoking probably reaches its peak in the thirty-five-to-forty age group. In the the over sixty-fives only about 23 percent of the men and 10 percent of the women smoke (this latter figure is now on the rise, as more and more young women are starting to smoke, and there are plenty of data to show that women have a much harder time kicking the habit than men). In one study, done in Newton, Massachusetts, the researchers report that "women, particularly Jewish women, may soon overtake men in the number who smoke."

There are more blue-collar smokers than white-collar smokers, and the unemployed smoke more than the employed. Smokers change jobs more often than nonsmokers. The higher the job level, the fewer the smokers. This links up with another fact: the higher the education level, the fewer the smokers.

There are many more white heavy smokers (over a pack a day) than there are blacks. This is true of both men and women.

Divorced and widowed people smoke more than the married, but those who have never married smoke least. Among religious groups, Catholics (whose church has been more tolerant toward smoking than the Protestant denominations) are the heaviest smokers.

People who live on farms smoke less than their neighbors in small villages and towns, who smoke considerably less than city dwellers.

Probably more important than the social aspects are the psychological differences between smokers and nonsmokers. There is ample proof, for example, that smokers are much more extroverted than nonsmokers. Heavy smokers are more extroverted than medium smokers, medium smokers more extroverted than ex-smokers, and both nonsmokers and pipe smokers are the least extroverted. Some studies indicate that smokers are more interested in TV and movies and are more active in sports. But there are also studies that show that nonsmokers are also active in sports. The apparent contradiction may be the result of not separating types of sports. Football and other team sports would appeal more to the gregarious smoker, while swimming and tennis attract the more introverted, nonsmoking types.

On the other hand, nonsmokers show more participation in organizations, hold more offices, and are more studious and more likely to read books.

It's possible that a person smokes because he's extroverted. It's also entirely possible that his extroversion leads him into activities where he is more likely to be stimulated to smoke—and perhaps extroverts are more susceptible to social influences.

There is also a clear indication that smokers are more

neurotic than nonsmokers; neuroticism being defined through psychological tests and by anxiety, nervousness, and unusual restlessness in terms of changing jobs and residences. The more neurotic and emotionally disturbed a person is, the more likely it is that he will inhale. There is a connection between feelings of tension, in many people, and a sensation of craving in the chest. This is satisfied by inhaling smoke, a reaction that some researchers have called "pulmonary eroticism," a deliberate irritation of the lungs to soothe the savage breast.

The true inside picture of the smoker is generally the exact opposite of the Marlboro cowboy or the Virginia Slim sophisticate, according to a study of six hundred male and female cigarette smokers in Toronto, Canada. Men smokers were usually affected by their feelings, shy and imaginative (as well as in poor physical condition), while the women were unusually assertive, opinionated, forthright, and self-sufficient (and in relatively good shape). The investigators think that "smoking is actually linked with a dependent, feminine character in men, and with aggressive masculine characteristics in women." *

They also found some other interesting nonsexual personality traits. The men were characterized by unusual tension and lack of self-discipline. The women were tender minded, dependent, emotionally unstable, shy, apprehensive, lacking in self-discipline, and overly tense.

These authors feel that it is worth emphasizing these findings. "If the smoker can be shown he is revealing his weakness by lighting a cigarette, then not only will the external reinforcement of his habit be destroyed, but smoking may become an aversive act, leading to a rapid extinction of the conditioned reflex of the habit smoker."

* Shephard, Rode, and Ross, "Reinforcement of a Smoking Withdrawal Program." *Canadian Journal of Public Health* 64 (March/April 1973): S47.

DAYS TWO THROUGH TEN

Tobacco was not known in the
Golden Age. So much the worse
for the Golden Age.

William Cowper
Letter to William Bull

These are Action Days. Each Day has its own Actions.
These are to be read and followed one Day at a time.

DAY TWO | *Action*

What Kind of Smoker Are You?

A lone man's companion, a bachelor's friend, a
hungry man's food, a sad man's cordial, a wakeful man's sleep, and a chilly man's fire. Sir;
while for stanching of wounds, purging of rheum,
and settling of the stomach, there's no herb
like unto it under the canopy of heaven.

Charles Kingsley
Westward Ho

Before you even think about trying to quit you must know
why you smoke. Take the test below. It will help you know
what you get out of smoking.

The test consists of statements made by different people
to describe what smoking means to them. Do you feel this
way—and, if so, how often? This is what counts. Circle one
number for each statement.

IMPORTANT: Answer Every Question.

	AL- WAYS	FRE- QUENTLY	OCCASION- ALLY	SEL- DOM	NEVER
A. I smoke cigarettes in order to keep myself from slowing down.	5	4	3	2	1

	ALWAYS	FREQUENTLY	OCCASIONALLY	SELDOM	NEVER
B. Handling a cigarette is part of the enjoyment of smoking it.	(5)	4	3	2	1
C. Smoking cigarettes is pleasant and relaxing.	5	(4)	3	2	1
D. I light a cigarette when I feel angry about something.	(5)	4	3	2	1
E. When I have run out of cigarettes I find it almost unbearable until I can get some more.	5	4	3	2	1
F. I smoke cigarettes automatically, without even being aware of it.	5	(4)	3	2	1
G. I smoke cigarettes to stimulate me, to perk myself up.	(5)	4	3	2	1
H. Part of the enjoyment of smoking a cigarette comes from the steps I take to light up.	5	4	3	2	(1)
I. I find cigarettes pleasurable.	5	4	(3)	2	1

	AL- WAYS	FRE- QUENTLY	OCCASION- ALLY	SEL- DOM	NEVER
J. When I feel uncomfortable or upset about something, I light a cigarette.	5	4	3	2	1
K. I am uncomfortably aware of when I am not smoking a cigarette.	5	4	3	2	1
L. I light a cigarette without realizing I still have one burning in the ashtray.	5	4	3	2	1
M. I smoke cigarettes to give me a lift.	5	4	3	2	1
N. When I smoke a cigarette, part of the enjoyment is watching the smoke as I exhale it.	5	4	3	2	1
O. I want a cigarette most when I am comfortable and relaxed.	5	4	3	2	1
P. When I feel blue or want to take my mind off cares and worries, I smoke cigarettes.	5	4	3	2	1
Q. I get a real gnawing hunger for a cigarette when I haven't smoked for a while.	5	4	3	2	1

	AL-WAYS	FRE-QUENTLY	OCCASION-ALLY	SEL-DOM	NEVER
R. I've found a cigarette in my mouth and didn't remember putting it there.	5	4	3	2	(1)

How to Score Yourself:

1. Enter the numbers you have circled to the questions in the spaces below, putting the number you circled for Question A on the line above A, the number you circled for Question B on line B, and so on.

2. Add the three numbers on each line across, from left to right, and write the totals at the end of that line above the words "Stimulation," "Handling," etc. These words describe the main reasons why most people smoke. The score at the end of each line, above each word, can be from three to fifteen. Any score of eleven or more is a high score. Any score of seven and below is low for that particular category.

				Totals
4	5	5	= 14	
A	**G**	**M**		Stimulation
5	1	3	= 9	
B	**H**	**N**		Handling
4	3	3	= 10	
C	**I**	**O**		Pleasurable Relaxation
5	5	5	= 15	
D	**J**	**P**		Crutch: Tension Reduction
5	4	5	= 14	
E	**K**	**Q**		Craving: Psychological Addiction
4	1	1	= 6	
F	**L**	**R**		Habit

Now, to learn what your score means, read on.

This test is designed to give you your score in each of six factors.

You may smoke for only one of these reasons. Or you may have several high scores, which means you have more than one reason for smoking. Everybody smokes for a different reason or combination of reasons, and it is quite usual for smoking to become involved with more than one type of satisfaction or requirement.

Three of these factors are positive.

1) **Stimulation.** A high score here indicates that you get a sense of increased energy from smoking. Such people are likely to begin the day with a cigarette. Do you take a cigarette when you feel you must keep yourself from slowing down? Do you feel good when you smoke and bad when you don't?

2) **Handling.** Something to do with your hands; the satisfaction of manipulating things. Do you make a ritual out of the physical touching and selecting of a cigarette? Do you use a cigarette case? A lighter? Do you have a set way of lighting up? Do you enjoy watching the smoke as you exhale?

3) **Relaxation.** Millions of smokers (15 percent of the total) will tell you that a cigarette relaxes them. This is because, as we have seen, they have learned to smoke a cigarette at a time when they are relaxed.

Such folk are likely to want a cigarette with their lunchtime or evening cocktail, after a meal, after sex. In a way, they are using cigarettes to reward themselves, by enhancing pleasurable feelings with a smoke.

The other three factors are negative.

4) **Tension reduction.** This is more than mere pleasurable relaxation. It is the management of unpleasant feelings such as tension, anxiety, anger, and shame by means of a cigarette. This characterizes the largest category of smokers. At least 30 percent are tension or "crutch" smokers.

Some questions you can ask yourself are: Do you light a cigarette when you are angry or depressed or anxious? When a tough problem comes up, do you automatically reach for a cigarette? Does smoking somehow help to smooth out the rough spots in your life?

5) **Need.** This is a complex pattern of rising and falling craving for a cigarette. Do you look forward to your next cigarette before you've finished the one you're smoking? Do you chain smoke—light one from the butt of the other? Do you feel that there is something missing from your life any time you are not actually smoking?—that you can't go to sleep if you run out of cigarettes, because it would be impossible to wake up in a house without a smoke? Is the time between each cigarette a period of rising tension that you can only release by lighting up?

Do you feel hooked on cigarettes?

About one out of every four smokers really craves cigarettes and is so strongly habituated to smoking that he will not only walk but if necessary swim or crawl a mile to get a pack. But this doesn't mean that he can't get that monkey off his back.

6) **Habit.** Although all cigarette smoking is habitual, the habit smoker, in this sense, is someone who often smokes without knowing it. The late President Dwight D. Eisenhower was like this. One day, when he caught himself setting fire to a cigarette while a freshly lit one was burning in his ashtray, he got so mad that he quit smoking. The habit smoker has been smoking for so long that the connection between smoking and feelings, either positive or negative, has become blurred or lost.

Habit smokers should ask: Do you find yourself smoking without wanting a cigarette, or particularly needing one? Do you smoke automatically, without satisfaction? Do you find yourself smoking more and enjoying it less? Do you sometimes find that you have lit two cigarettes?

DAY THREE | *Action*

The List

Tobacco is a filthy weed,
That from the Devil does proceed;
It drains your purse, it burns your clothes,
And makes a chimney of your nose.

Benjamin Waterhouse

Write down a list of reasons for wanting to give up smoking.
Here are some taken from a blackboard at a recent meeting
of a California group who are working together on quitting:

They burn my clothes.
They burn the furniture.
Dirty fingers.
Bad example to the children.
Smell up the room.
Make me smell bad.
Not able to concentrate as well when smoking.
Cost too much.

Add your own reasons, and concentrate on the positive
benefits—living longer, feeling better, smelling nicer, personal satisfaction in mastering a habit (once you do this,
you'll find you can handle others, too). Reread the list

daily and add to it. Finally, boil it down to two or three key reasons that mean the most to you. Write these on a card, and carry the card with you. Look at it every time you want a cigarette—whether you smoke one or not.

DAY FOUR | *Action*

The Wrap Sheet

They (the Huron Indians) believe that
there is nothing so suitable as Tobacco to
appease the passions; that is why they never
attend a council without a pipe or calumet in
their mouths. The smoke, they say, gives them
intelligence, and enables them to see clearly
through the most intricate matters.

> Jean de Brebeuf
> *17th-Century French explorer*

Here's a very simple experiment that will reveal a great deal
more about your smoking. It has worked for literally thousands of smokers.

Take the form on the following page and reproduce it,
either with a pencil and ruler or on a photocopy machine,
to equal the number of packs of cigarettes you smoke in a
week. Seven packs require seven sheets, fourteen packs,
fourteen sheets, and so on.

Now, during the next week smoke as much as you want
to. But wrap each package in one of these "wrap sheets."

Secure the wrap sheet with two elastic bands around your package.

Each time you want to smoke, unwrap your package and take the cigarette. But mark on the sheet, as indicated, the information requested: the number of that cigarette out of the pack, the time of day you smoked it, what you were doing at the time, how you were feeling (lively, tired, happy, depressed, etc.), how badly you needed that particular cigarette. Then write down a reason for quitting. Then fill in one of the final two spaces, depending on whether you decided to smoke or not to smoke the cigarette. There's no shame or guilt attached to the decision that you *did* want to smoke and *did* smoke—that's normal.

The purpose of this test isn't to make you stop smoking, but to make you understand a bit more of how you feel about smoking and to make you aware of when you are smoking.

It is a revelation to most people.

Harold, a thirty-five-year-old hospital technician in Anaheim, California, said, "I was smoking thirty cigarettes a day. When I finished doing my wrap sheet for one day, I realized that half of those cigarettes were after cups of coffee. I had never realized that I was drinking so much coffee —and that I always smoked after each cup. Fifteen cups of coffee is enough to make anyone nervous. I immediately began cutting down on my coffee—set a limit of five cups a day—and that eliminated ten cigarettes."

After having chopped his smoke intake by a third, Harold was able to figure out that most of his other smokes weren't really needed, either. In a few days he'd cut his habit in half, and then he began systematically weeding out the weeds he could do without, until he was down to three a day. It was comparatively easy to drop those—and he's been off cigarettes for six months now.

Anna, an attractive thirty-year-old housewife of Fresno, found that the wrap sheet was a real icebreaker at a party.

D A I L Y   C I G A R E T T E   C O U N T

INSTRUCTIONS: Wrap this "Daily Cigarette Count" around your pack of cigarettes and hold it fast with two rubber bands. Complete the information below if you unwrap your pack or are offered a cigarette by someone else.

Day of the Week _____ Date _____ Pack Number of the Day _____

Cigarette (circle)	Time of the Day	Activity	Feeling	Need Rating* (circle)	Reason for Quitting	I decide to: Smoke/Not Smoke This Cigarette	
1				1 2 3 4 5		( )	( )
2				1 2 3 4 5		( )	( )
3				1 2 3 4 5		( )	( )
4				1 2 3 4 5		( )	( )
5				1 2 3 4 5		( )	( )
6				1 2 3 4 5		( )	( )
7				1 2 3 4 5		( )	( )
8				1 2 3 4 5		( )	( )
9				1 2 3 4 5		( )	( )
10				1 2 3 4 5		( )	( )
11				1 2 3 4 5		( )	( )
12				1 2 3 4 5		( )	( )
13				1 2 3 4 5		( )	( )
14				1 2 3 4 5		( )	( )
15				1 2 3 4 5		( )	( )
16				1 2 3 4 5		( )	( )
17				1 2 3 4 5		( )	( )
18				1 2 3 4 5		( )	( )
19				1 2 3 4 5		( )	( )
20				1 2 3 4 5		( )	( )

Need Rating: How important that particular cigarette is to you at the time.

      1—Most important (would have missed it very much)
      2—Above average
      3—Average
      4—Below average
      5—Least important (would not have missed it)

Courtesy: American Cancer Society
      Smoking Education Project

She had always been rather shy with strangers. But when she took out her pack at a cocktail party and began unwrapping and marking the paper, a number of people she didn't know at all gathered around, fascinated. They began asking questions and she found herself explaining what she was up to. "Before I knew it, I was the center of attention," Anna said later. "People kept coming up to me and asking to see my cigarettes. And everybody was talking about this trick. And I was so busy explaining, I didn't have much time to smoke."

Normally, Anna loved to smoke when she was having a drink. Usually, at a party she finished a full pack. But that night she couldn't manage to smoke more than eight cigarettes. She dates her victory over smoking from that party.

Fred is a fortyish stockbroker. When he started wrapping his cigarettes, he was smoking four packs—eighty cigarettes —a day. "I had the notion that I was a habit smoker," he says today, "but the wrap sheet proved it to me in twenty-four hours. I realized that more than half the cigarettes I was burning I didn't even know I had lit. If you figure ten minutes a cigarette, I was smoking eight hundred minutes a day—over thirteen hours. But nobody could smoke that much. You wouldn't have time to draw a breath of fresh air between cigarettes at that rate. I work in a pressure business. I was smoking unconsciously. What I was doing was lighting them and putting them down—or holding one without realizing it—the holes in my clothes could tell you that. I don't think I consciously smoked—actually smoked—a pack a day."

The wrap sheet gave him the boost he needed. His children (ages eight and ten) had been after him for months to quit smoking—they were worried about his health, from what they'd learned in school. The burns in his suits bothered him. And he had a sneaking suspicion that his breath and clothing reeked of the odor of smoke. "I only realized how bad I smelled a few weeks after I quit and my sense of smell came back," he says now. Eventually, he kicked his four-pack-a-day habit and has never looked back. "I'll never smoke again," he says.

DAY FIVE | *Action*

What Do You Think About Smoking?
(Continue to wrap your cigarettes and to mark all spaces in the wrap sheet.)

A custom loathsome to the eye, hateful to the
nose, harmful to the brain, dangerous to the
lungs, and in the black, stinking fume thereof
nearest resembling the horrible Stygian smoke
of the pit that is bottomless.

> James I of England
> *A Counterblaste to Tobacco*

Probably the most important reason—important to most
people—for quitting cigarettes is health. Even if you aren't
worried about the health risks of smoking, it will be worth-
while for you to take the following test on what you *believe*
the effects of smoking are.

For each statement, circle the number that shows most
closely how you feel about it—do you strongly agree, mildly
agree, mildly disagree, or strongly disagree?

Again, it's important to answer every question.

	STRONGLY AGREE	MILDLY AGREE	MILDLY DISAGREE	STRONGLY DISAGREE
A. Cigarette smoking is not nearly as dangerous as many other health hazards.	1	2	3	4

	STRONGLY AGREE	MILDLY AGREE	MILDLY DISAGREE	STRONGLY DISAGREE
B. I don't smoke enough to get any of the diseases that cigarette smoking is supposed to cause.	1	(2)	3	4
C. If a person has already smoked for many years, it probably won't do him much good to stop.	1	2	3	(4)
D. It would be hard for me to give up smoking cigarettes.	(1)	2	3	4
E. Cigarette smoking is enough of a health hazard for something to be done about it.	(4)	3	2	1
F. The kind of cigarette I smoke is much less likely than other kinds to give me any of the diseases that smoking is supposed to cause.	1	2	3	(4)
G. As soon as a person quits smoking cigarettes he begins to recover from much of the damage that smoking has caused.	(4)	3	2	1
H. It would be hard for me to cut down to half the number of cigarettes I now smoke.	(1)	2	3	4

	STRONGLY AGREE	MILDLY AGREE	MILDLY DISAGREE	STRONGLY DISAGREE
I. The whole problem of cigarette smoking and health is a very minor one.	1	2	3	(4)
J. I haven't smoked long enough to worry about the diseases that cigarette smoking is supposed to cause.	1	2	3	(4)
K. Quitting smoking helps a person to live longer.	(4)	3	2	1
L. It would be difficult for me to make any substantial changes in my smoking habits.	1	(2)	3	4

How to Score Yourself:

1. Enter in the spaces below the numbers you have circled, putting the number you have circled to Question A over line A, to Question B over line B, etc.

2. Total the three scores across on each line to find your totals. For example, the sum of your scores over lines A, E, and I gives you your score on Importance; lines B, F, and J give the score on Personal Relevance, etc.

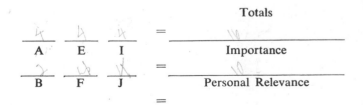

				Totals
4	4	4	=	10
A	E	I		Importance
2	2	4	=	10
B	F	J		Personal Relevance
			=	

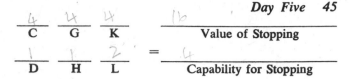

4	4	4	16	
C	G	K		Value of Stopping
1	1	2	= 4	
D	H	L		Capability for Stopping

Although your answers have been placed in four vertical columns, to find your score you must add horizontally across, then place the total for each three answers on the line at right. Thus, you will have four scores, for Importance, Personal Relevance, Value of Stopping, and Capability for Stopping. These scores can vary from three to twelve. Any score of nine or more is high; six or below is low.

Importance. A high score shows that you know about the overall dangers of smoking. Chances are, however, that even if you are aware of the hazards, you do not know how serious they really are—that one pack a day at age twenty-five reduces life expectancy by more than eight years, as an example. Suggested reading: Day Six, "Do You Know What Happens When You Smoke?" and the Appendix, an update on the specific diseases and other conditions caused by continued smoking.

If you score low in this category, it may be that you do not believe that your health is important to you. Some people think that they feel this way, until they become seriously ill. Or, more likely, you may not know all the facts about health and smoking. In any case, you may learn something from the readings mentioned above. Read them, and see if your score doesn't go up.

Personal Relevance. If you score high, you have a strong motive for giving up cigarettes.

If you score low, you may believe, like many, that "it's only statistics," and you won't be one of them. You may also have the idea that you have to smoke a great deal for many more years before smoking begins to harm you.

Unfortunately, this is not so. Read Day Six. This tells

you what happens to every smoker—no exceptions—with every cigarette. It's not a matter of statistics, but a matter of simple pharmacology, the effects of nicotine and the several thousand other elements of tobacco smoke on *your* body, no matter how young or old you are.

If you're a young smoker, you should know that even a few years of regular smoking can damage your breathing capacity, handicapping sports performance, at the very least. Even if you smoke only a half-pack a day, your risk of dying young is considerably increased.

Benefits of Stopping: Just as there are immediate and daily health threats in smoking, there are quick and increasing benefits from quitting. We will go into these in detail later on, but lung capacity in the young smoker improves markedly after a few weeks of nonsmoking. The danger of heart attack—the major cause of smoking-related deaths— drops sharply within a year of nonsmoking. Then there are the immediate esthetic and economic benefits—sweeter breath, no tobacco odor in clothes or furniture, no new cigarette burns, the daily money saved on cigarettes.

There are health advantages even for long-term smokers who quit before any symptoms or impairment occur. Their chance of serious illness drops with passing months and their death rate drops, too, until it eventually approaches that of people who have never smoked.

Of course, people with bad hearts or those who have had heart attacks or who have chronic stomach ulcers and respiratory diseases such as emphysema and chronic bronchitis should definitely quit smoking. They have no choice, if they want to avoid becoming invalids or suffering early death.

Capability for Stopping. If you score high here, no problem. If you score six or below, you believe that it will be difficult for you to quit. But you may be encouraged by the fact that among quitters are those with every kind of motive for smoking, with every variety of habit—from the most hard-core to the least habituated—every age group, both sexes, and all national and ethnic backgrounds. If you could meet them all, you would find a number like yourself, who thought they couldn't quit, but did.

Review Your Scores. Before you attempt to quit smoking, you must believe more than the warning label on the package. You must be aware of the importance of the smoking problem—its importance to you personally. You have to be convinced that there are both immediate and long-term benefits from stopping. And, most of all, you have to believe that you *can* quit.

Do You Know What Happens When You Smoke?
(Continue wrapping your cigarettes.)

Tobacco surely was designed
To poison and destroy mankind.

> Philip Freneau
> *Tobacco*

Do You Know What Happens When You Smoke?

Here are ten questions to help you answer the query above.
All you have to do is circle the right answer. There may be
more than one right answer to some questions. Circle as
many as you think correct.

QUESTIONS	ANSWERS
1. If you inhale tobacco smoke, how much of the smoke stays in your body: Up to . . .	a) 10% b) 25% c) 50% d) 90%
2. What gives cigarette smoke that country-fresh flavor?	a) propane b) butane c) formaldehyde d) hydrogen cyanide
3. Your blood has how many times as much affinity for carbon monoxide as for oxygen?	a) 10 b) 50 c) 100 d) 200

QUESTIONS	ANSWERS
4. How high is cigarette country?	a) 500 feet b) 1,000 feet c) a mile d) 8,000 feet
5. Nicotine gives you a lift. What does it lift, actually?	a) your blood pressure b) your heartbeat c) number of irregular heartbeats d) oxygen consumption of heart
6. What advantages do smoking mothers give their children?	a) miscarriage b) infant death c) underweight d) retarded learning
7. How many annual United States deaths from heart attack come from cigarettes?	a) 100 b) 1,000 c) 100,000 d) 188,000
8. How much tar does a pack-a-day smoker inhale in a year?	a) 1 ounce b) 2 ounces c) 4 ounces d) 8 ounces
9. How many chemicals in cigarette smoke cause cancer?	a) none b) 5 c) 15 d) 30
10. What's worse than lung cancer?	a) nothing b) chronic bronchitis c) emphysema d) housemaid's knee

How to Score Yourself

Count the number of correct answers at the end of this chapter, after reading this chapter. There are twenty correct answers to the ten questions. Thus, a score of twenty is perfect—anyone who scores this high has a very good idea of the harm that smoking does each time he inhales a cigarette. Fifteen is a good score, ten is fair, five poor. This is one quiz where nobody loses; but, since a high grade can only aid you in your resolve to quit smoking, we suggest you take the test over and over until you get a perfect score. The real prize is better health. Now, read to learn the facts.

Dr. Fredrickson tells the story of one of his friends, a man in his thirties, who smoked three and a half packs of cigarettes a day. When the "Surgeon General's Report on Smoking and Health" came out in 1964, he temporarily cut down on his cigarettes. But he was soon smoking as much as ever. His reasoning: "I somehow had the feeling that this just didn't apply to me. After all, I was in excellent health even though I smoked very heavily."

Early one morning he was awakened from a sound sleep by a jolting chest pain which he thought was a heart attack. During the emergency room examination the doctor casually asked whether he smoked, and suggested that he might want to think about quitting. The pain turned out to be not a coronary but a collapsed lung. But the man stopped smoking anyhow. Somehow, in his mind, he said later, there was a connection between the pain and cigarettes, and whatever pleasure he was getting from smoking "just wasn't worth it."

In young people, the health threat in smoking seems very far off. After all, it takes years to develop a serious disease, and they can always quit, can't they?

John A. Yacenda, who runs a smoking withdrawal clinic for the Ventura, California, health department, says that the question asked most often by teen-agers is "how long does it take for smoking to harm you?"

Yacenda's reply: "About three seconds." Or less. In the tiny interval after you light up, drag on a cigarette, and inhale, that rich country flavor goes to work—on your heart, your lungs, your whole body. It raises your blood pressure by ten to twenty points, starts your heart pounding up to an extra twenty-five beats per minute, lowers your skin temperature, and dims your eyesight. It corrodes the delicate membranes of your lips, your tongue, your palate; it hacks at your throat, rasps your vocal cords, claws your windpipe. In your lungs it chokes the airways and rots the gossamer air sacs, leaving a residue of cancer-causing chemicals. It deposits these and other dangerous poisons in your stomach, kidneys, and bladder. It even insinuates toxins into your pancreas. All of this happens with every cigarette you smoke. No smoker is immune.

When you exhale, up to 90 percent of that true tobacco taste stays with you in the form of hundreds of millions of submicroscopic particles of twelve hundred chemicals, whose toxic interactions are so numerous they are nearly immeasurable. In this balanced blend of fine aromas are acids, glycerol, glycol, alcohols, aldehydes, ketones, aliphatic hydrocarbons, aromatic hydrocarbons, and phenols —most of which you'll find in the smoke of your chimney or your automobile exhaust. None is a health food and many will do you harm.

Most doctors have known for years, from treating smokers, that cigarette smoke causes a variety of diseases. Some scientists scoffed, however; it wasn't possible that one substance, smoke, could attack so many parts of the body in so many ways. But research has shown that tobacco smoke isn't a single substance. Sixty percent of what you inhale into your lungs is gas, a dozen different noxious vapors, the main ones being propane, butane, methane, formaldehyde, methanol, acetone, ammonia, and hydrogen cyanide. And now science is zeroing in on one that's even deadlier: colorless, odorless, lethal, carbon monoxide.

Present in cigarette smoke in a concentration of six hundred and forty times the safe level in industrial plants, this insidious poison has two hundred times the affinity for your red blood cells that life-giving oxygen does. Those cells are designed to carry oxygen throughout your body. When you smoke, as many as 15 percent of your blood cells are transporting life-denying carbon monoxide in place of vital oxygen.

In a nonsmoker, the normal level of blood carbon monoxide is less than 1 percent. In the lungs of a two-pack-a-day smoker, the carbon monoxide concentration is a steady 50 ppm. Thus, the air inside his lungs exceeds the permissible limits of carbon monoxide in outside air considered safe for people to breathe.

Carbon monoxide lasts a lot longer than the rich aroma. Its "half-life" in the blood is about three to four hours, so it takes a good eight-hour sleep to rid yourself of three quarters of the carbon monoxide (that is, if you don't add to it by smoking in the middle of the night).

Carbon monoxide not only prevents the red cells from picking up enough oxygen; it also inhibits those cells which do carry oxygen from giving it up as fast as your tissues demand it.

Because of carbon monoxide, cigarette country is always about eight thousand feet above sea level. A cigarette smoker who lives at zero altitude is breathing the oxygen-thin air of someone who is nearly two miles in the clouds. It's why every smoker who is a sportsman finds himself out of breath quicker than his nonsmoking competitors.

There's no age limit on the effect. A teen-age smoker will feel the lack of oxygen under mild stress even if he smokes only five or six cigarettes per day. And this is only one of the less deadly results of carbon monoxide, particularly when its effects are added to those of nicotine.

It's the nicotine that gives you a lift. It lifts your blood pressure, your heartbeat and your cardiac output (the amount of blood pumped by your heart), as well as stroke volume, velocity of contraction, contractile force, and oxygen consumption of the heart muscle. It increases the irregular heartbeats and the changes in electrocardiogram and ballistocardiogram. It does this by releasing three substances known as catecholamines (the main one is adrenalin) from your tissues into your nervous system. The catecholamines push your heart so hard it requires more blood in its coronary arteries to keep up with the demand. Healthy hearts rise to the occasion. But in people with coronary artery disease, the hard-working heart doesn't get enough additional blood. As a matter of fact, one stress test that doctors sometimes use to detect coronary artery disease is to ask smoking patients to smoke a cigarette. If they get chest pains, the test is positive.

New studies show that nicotine and carbon monoxide cross the "placental barrier," so that a pregnant woman who smokes is smoking for two. The nicotine constricts the blood vessels in her unborn child, cutting down on fetal blood flow. Carbon monoxide reduces the amount of oxygen in the reduced blood supply. Thus, the fetus just can't get enough blood or oxygen to grow as fast as normal. This may be why the children of mothers who smoke during pregnancy weigh an average of six ounces less at birth than the babies of non-smoking mothers. Smoking mothers as a group also have more miscarriages and stillbirths, and their babies are more likely to die in the first month after birth. Their babies don't grow as fast, and as late as age seven are smaller and some-what behind children of nonsmoking mothers in school (See Appendix).

The adrenalin released by nicotine hits fat cells all over your body, causing them to pour their tiny globules of fat, known as lipids, generously into your blood. The lipid you've probably heard most about is cholesterol. Every time you smoke your blood cholesterol goes up, and a high level of lipids in the blood is known to be directly related to the onset of artery disease.

In some unexplained way, smoking seems to affect the coronary arteries. Both in men smokers and in dogs that had been taught to smoke cigarettes, the arteries in the heart muscle were thicker than those in comparable nonsmokers; the thickness increased with the number of cigarettes per day and with age. Autopsy studies showed that hardening of the arteries is more common and severe among smokers, and it increases in relation to the use of cigarettes.

Smoking doesn't cause all the heart attacks in this coun-try. But scientists calculate that cigarettes are responsible for about 188,000 of the one million deaths from heart and artery disease each year in the United States. These are called "excess deaths" that need not have occurred if those people hadn't smoked; they occur mostly in people in their forties and fifties.

Cigarettes are cooling, even without menthol. As soon as you inhale, your skin temperature begins to drop by as much as six degrees Fahrenheit. The reason is that those same catecholamines, released by nicotine, cause spasms to grip the tiny arteries that supply your skin and extremities, constricting circulation. The effect is only temporary. But since it happens puff after puff, if you puff long enough, the temporary effects may add up to chronic injury when combined with hardened arteries. This is what doctors call peripheral vascular disease. Long-distance circulation eventually may be permanently turned off, not supplying enough blood to fingers, toes, arms, or legs to keep them alive.

The reason your cigarette doesn't cop out on flavor is mainly the millions of particles of chemicals floating around in the visible part of smoke. Condensed, they form viscous, black, smelly "tar." A Swedish scientist estimates that a pack-a-day smoker inhales a full cup, eight ounces, of tar in the course of a year. Inhalers gulp tar directly through their mouths into their lungs. The lungs have their defenses: mucus, which traps dirt and microbes; cilia, tiny hairlike structures lining the airways, beating steadily to move the mucus toward the throat; and macrophages, vacuum-cleaner cells that hustle around, gathering and neutralizing harmful substances.

Cigarette smoke slows down and eventually stops the cilia while causing spasms and swelling in the air passages. The effect is to choke off the smaller bronchi with mucus. And smoke cancels the macrophages' ability to neutralize foreign matter.

In tar, against which your lungs' defenses are neutralized, are about thirty chemicals that cause cancer. Several are "complete carcinogens," which means that they can cause malignant tumors all by themselves. Others are "tumor initiators" and "tumor promoters" that need each other to start a cancer. A recently discovered class of compounds in cigarette smoke is "cancer accelerators." After the others have begun a cancer, they come along and give it a rocketlike boost to turn it into a full-fledged tumor.

One chemical in tar, beta-naphthylamine, is a specific cause of bladder cancer in human beings, so powerful that many countries have restricted its manufacture (it's used in dyes). A researcher calculates that 35 percent of bladder cancers in the United States are caused by cigarettes, resulting in thirty-one hundred unnecessary deaths a year from this comparatively rare disease.

But, says the Surgeon General, tar is a more powerful cancer-causing agent than the sum of its part. Wherever it touches tissue, it produces abnormal cells. These aren't cancer, but it is among these deformed cells that cancers start. In pipe and cigar smokers who generally don't inhale because the smoke is too alkaline for comfort, the common cancers occur where smoke touches: lip, tongue, mouth, larynx, and esophagus.

In cigarette smokers who inhale, cancers occur all along the route, with the most numerous being in the lung. Cigarette smokers also get more bladder and pancreas cancers. The main cause of cancer deaths in smokers is, however, from lung cancer, which is about 94 percent fatal. About sixty thousand of the seventy-two thousand annual United States deaths from lung cancer are caused by smoking cigarettes, according to the American Cancer Society. Most of the dead are men, but women, who have come a long way, baby, are beginning to catch up (see Appendix C).

Cigarettes cause other lung diseases, too, that permit you to smoke yourself to death more slowly. Most smokers know the delight of that first morning's coughing spell. It happens because during the night your anesthetized cilia begin to wake up and move the mucus. Under the microscope, a smoker's sputum shows tiny corkscrew shapes. These are, literally, dried mucus moldings of the small airways which they plugged while he was smoking. As smoking continues, mucus plugs larger airways, some of them as thick as your finger. The cough becomes chronic. Steady hacking and spitting are the symptoms of chronic bronchitis. Overproduction of mucus caused by this disease reduces the lungs' ability to fight off infection, and the mucus is an excellent breeding ground for infection, which is one reason why smokers get more colds. Chronic bronchitis can kill, too.

It has a steady companion known as pulmonary emphysema, a disease that destroys the air sacs in the lung. In normal lungs, there are 300 million of these tiny lung balloons, in which the air we breathe gives up its oxygen to the blood, which in turn rids itself of carbon dioxide and other wastes. The inner surfaces of these sacs are coated with a superthin layer of biological compounds (surfactants) whose surface tension aids the bellows action of the lungs. Cigarette smoke attacks this delicate layer. Scientists found that the surface tension of smokers' air sacs was far below normal, comparable with that of people with lung disease.

This is a short-term effect that returns to normal when you stop smoking. But scientists theorize that two things happen over the long term. Smoke attacks lung tissue, causing it to deteriorate and lose its breathing function. And the arteries of the lung are constricted by catecholamines, shutting off the blood supply so the tissue dies. A lung with emphysema looks like a piece of shredded silk, with loose threads in place of solid surface.

Recently, a pathologist studied the lungs of more than eighteen hundred men and women who died of all causes. He classified them by the amount of emphysema. Then he compared the results with the carefully researched smoking histories of these people. More than 99 percent of the heavy smokers (more than a pack a day) had the disease, and in 19 percent it was very far advanced; but 90 percent of the nonsmokers had no emphysema, and there wasn't a single advanced case among them. Even among coal miners and other workers exposed to lung-damaging dust, severe emphysema is confined almost entirely to cigarette smokers.

"Lung cancer is a comparatively merciful death," says one doctor. "With emphysema you start gasping, and you may gasp for fifteen years." It creeps up on smokers. We all start with about one hundred square yards of interior lung surface, but almost never do we need it all. Most of us live our lives on about 20 percent of our lung capacity. The first hint a smoker has of emphysema is when he gets out of breath after a small exertion, like running for a bus. He may think this is an early warning; it isn't. It means that most of his lung reserve has been destroyed. A bad cold may hospitalize him.

Even when warned, many smokers bravely refuse to quit. Visit the respiratory ward of your local hospital and you'll see them, never more than a few yards from their oxygen tanks and respirators. Their entire life is devoted to one thing: breathing. Ask one how he is and he gasps, "Fine."

The doctor says, "You don't sound fine."

"This (gasp) is a (gasp) good day."

The Surgeon General says that cigarettes are the most important cause of emphysema and chronic bronchitis in this country. These diseases kill more than thirty thousand United States residents a year (see Appendix D).

The list of smoking-related diseases is long. Smokers have more gastric ulcers than nonsmokers and take longer to heal; more periodontal disease, which attacks teeth and gums; and more trench mouth (see Appendix E). And evidence is accumulating to show that cigarette smoke attacks the central nervous system.

The damage is "dose related." Each cigarette does some harm. Each additional smoke repeats the insult. Eventually, these incessant attacks on the body may turn into disease. The break-even point for lung cancer is about one million puffs, or one hundred thousand cigarettes—a pack a day for fifteen years—when the daily impairments may edge into irreversible disease. Since smoking effects are cumulative, it isn't the one hundred-thousandth cigarette that does the damage, but the combined effects of the previous 99,999. There's no safe level of smoking but, since the harm is dose related, research shows that cutting down on the number of cigarettes, and smoking those with efficient filters that give off less tar and nicotine, reduce the risk of serious illness. But a heavy smoker even of filtered cigarettes still has five times the risk of lung cancer of a nonsmoker, according to a recent study at Roswell Park Memorial Institute in Buffalo, New York.

The real payoff comes from quitting. Unless an irreversible disease has set in, when you stop smoking you'll notice that, first off, your chronic bronchitis will begin to clear up. No more hacking and coughing. Fewer colds. A cleaner mouth—and breath. Even your clothes and your home will smell better. Your ulcers may improve. Stay off cigarettes for a year and you begin to move out of the lung cancer danger zone. Lung tissue destroyed by smoking does not regenerate. But when you stop assaulting your lungs with smoke that tastes good like a cigarette should, whatever breathing capacity you have left, you'll *keep*.

(*N.B.:* This chapter deals mainly with the immediate pathological effects of smoking. For more detailed information about the long-term serious disabilities and diseases, and deaths caused by smoking, see the Appendix.)

CORRECT ANSWERS

1. (d) 2. (a,b,c,d) 3. (d) 4. (d) 5. (a,b,c,d) 6. (a,b,c,d) 7. (d)
8. (d) 9. (d) 10. (b,c)

DAY SEVEN | *Action*

Do You Want to Change Your Smoking Habits?
(Continue to wrap your cigarettes and fill out the wrap sheet before each.)

Pernicious weed! whose scent the fair annoys,
Unfriendly to Society's chief joys,
Thy worst effect is banishing for hours
The sex whose presence civilizes ours.

> William Cowper
> *Conversation*

Of course you want to change, or you would not have read this far in a book devoted to helping people quit. But it's useful to crystalize your reasons for wanting to change, because these play a vital part in whether you do or do not decide to quit. And that's what this test will help you do.

To take the test, indicate by circling the appropriate numbers how you feel about the following statements.

It's important to answer all the questions.

	COM-PLETELY AGREE	SOME-WHAT AGREE	SOME-WHAT DISAGREE	COM-PLETELY DISAGREE
A. Cigarette smoking might give me a serious illness.	(4)	3	2	1

	COM-PLETELY AGREE	SOME-WHAT AGREE	SOME-WHAT DISAGREE	COM-PLETELY DISAGREE
B. My cigarette smoking sets a bad example for others.	4	3	2	1
C. I find cigarette smoking to be a messy habit.	4	3	2	1
D. Controlling my cigarette smoking is a challenge to me.	4	3	2	1
E. Cigarettes are getting too expensive.	4	3	2	1
F. Smoking causes shortness of breath.	4	3	2	1
G. If I quit smoking cigarettes, it might influence others to stop.	4	3	2	1
H. Cigarettes burn my clothing, rugs, and furniture.	4	3	2	1
I. Quitting smoking would show that I can control myself.	4	3	2	1
J. I can use the money for something better.	4	3	2	1
K. My cigarette smoking will have a harmful effect on my health.	4	3	2	1
L. My cigarette smoking influences others close to me to take up or continue smoking.	4	3	2	1
M. If I quit smoking, my senses of taste and smell would improve.	4	3	2	1

	COMPLETELY AGREE	SOMEWHAT AGREE	SOMEWHAT DISAGREE	COMPLETELY DISAGREE
N. I do not like the idea of feeling dependent on smoking.	(4)	3	2	1
O. I could save a lot of money by not smoking.	4	(3)	2	1

How to Score Yourself

1. Enter the numbers you have circled to the questions on the blank lines below, putting the number you have circled for Question A over line A, to Question B over line B, and so on.

2. Then add the three numbers on each horizontal row across, and write the total on the line at the right, which is above a word—"Health," "Example," "Esthetics," "Mastery," or "Economics."

Totals

A	F	K	=		Health
B	G	L	=		Example
C	H	M	=		Esthetics
D	I	N	=		Mastery
E	J	O	=		Economics

Each of the words describes a motive for quitting cigarettes. The total on each line can vary from a minimum of three to a maximum of twelve. If you have a total of nine or more on a line, this is a high score for this motive. Scores of six or less are below-average scores. Low scores mean relatively less strong motives than high scores.

Health. Most smokers today who read newspapers and watch TV and listen to radio know that cigarette smoking has been proved unhealthy. They see this repeated every time they take out a pack—"Warning: The Surgeon General Has Determined That Cigarette Smoking Is Dangerous to Your Health." So, if you score nine or more on the health question, you are with the great majority of smokers, and you have a strong motive to stop smoking.

If your score is six or below, either you don't believe the warning or you haven't been interested in it. Perhaps you think health is not important to you, either because you think it's "too late" or because you think that you can run between the statistics. Or you may be confused by the claims and counterclaims about health and smoking; if so, there is sufficient information in this book (Day Six and Appendix) to answer any question on this subject.

Example. Perhaps you are concerned less for yourself than because you feel that you are an example to someone. Perhaps you are a parent and don't want your children to start smoking. You know that telling kids today, "Do what I say, not what I do," doesn't go down very well. There is reason for concern, for as we have seen, research proves that parents' smoking is a very important element in children's starting. Or perhaps you are a doctor, vexed at providing a poor example for your patients. One hundred thousand American doctors have quit cigarettes in recent years. As the National Clearinghouse for Smoking and Health says, "Maybe they know something you don't." Or perhaps you are a teacher or a Scout leader, anyone that others look up to.

The "exemplar" role is the second strongest motive for wanting to give up cigarettes. If you score high here, you have a big edge on motivation. And if you score high in both Health and Example, you are going to find it rather easy to *decide* to quit smoking.

But, strangely, these two very strong motives for wanting to quit lead to a very low level of success in actually giving up smoking. Dr. Daniel Horn believes that a large part of this is due to the fact that people are stimulated to take an action that they aren't prepared to cope with, which leads to anxiety. The desire to quit feeds on the anxiety and is blocked by the inability to do something about it. The net result is that many people, though strongly motivated to quit, actually end up smoking more than ever.

That is why this book does not try to persuade you to give up smoking, but to provide you with the means to do so in 14 days, or in your own good time.

Esthetics. Many people are disturbed about their cigarette breath, the smell of smoke in their hair and clothing, stained fingers, dirty ashtrays, burned clothing and furniture, and the other unpleasant esthetic side effects of smoking.

One New Jersey woman was appalled when, after a few days in a hospital, during which she had not been able to smoke, she smelled her nurse's breath. The nurse was a heavy cigarette smoker. "My God," the patient said, "I began to wonder if my breath smelled as bad as hers." A Ventura, California, secretary told me, "I got tired of having people call me 'Sir' when I answered the telephone. My voice was so hoarse from cigarettes." She stopped smoking and was very pleased when in a few weeks her tones began to sound more contralto than baritone. If you score nine or more in Esthetics, you have a good motive to give up cigarettes.

Mastery. The fourth key motive in wanting to quit is "Mastery." A New York real estate executive said, "I don't like the idea of being dominated by a habit. I want to be in control." This feeling of being controlled, of not being their own master, bothers many smokers, but many don't realize it until they take the test. Then they decide to stop smoking. A doctor I know quit this way. He was coughing his way down Fifth Avenue in New York City one morning when he suddenly got so mad at himself that he took two unopened packs of cigarettes and a Dunhill lighter out of his pocket and dropped them into the nearest trash can. And he never smoked again. If you score nine or more in this category, you have uncovered a motive for quitting that can also reinforce other motives.

A man who lives in Quebec, Canada, says, "I had been smoking for fourteen years. One Sunday night I was going out for cigarettes. My wife said she needed milk for the kids' breakfast. I didn't have enough money for both and there was nowhere to cash a check late Sunday evening. The fact that I had to think about which to buy was, in my opinion, *sick*. I haven't had a smoke since."

Economics. There is a direct relationship between the amount that people smoke and the price of cigarettes. On an Army base where, tax free, a pack costs only about ten cents, smokers smoke about twice as much as on the national average. And there is proof that as cigarettes get more expensive in relation to other things, there is a definite fall-off at each rise in price.

Today a pack a day costs on the average in the United States about fifty cents a day, or $182.50 a year. That's $365 for two packs a day, which means that on an average income you have to earn at least $400 to support a forty-cigarette-a-day habit.

That's not as expensive as heroin, but is something to think about. Many people are doing just that and finding economics a strong motive for quitting. If you score nine or more, you may be one of these. (See Day Eight on "The Profit in Quitting," and look for the economic tips among the "Fifty Ways to Cut Down," Day Fourteen.)

An ex-smoker in Michigan prepares computer profiles of smokers. Smoker Robert S. Wisler reports in the Detroit *News,* "The thing that bothers me about my profile isn't the amount, 14,600 cigarettes a year. Not even that I'm cutting my life short—I've already disposed of 7.137 years. I admit I'm concerned that if I keep smoking at this rate, I can expect 5.3 pounds of tars to circulate through my respiratory system during the next 20 years. The profile says I've already spent $7,084 on cigarettes, and can expect to spend another $39,433 by age 65, assuming that cigarettes don't go above 70 cents a pack. What really bothers me, though, is the idea of being sick a disproportionate part of whatever life I have left."

The Profit in Quitting
(Continue wrapping your cigarettes.)

> What this country really needs is a good five-cent cigar.
>
> Thomas R. Marshall, *Remark,* while presiding over the U.S. Senate as vice president, during a debate on the needs of the country

In the eighteenth century an inexpensive process for distilling alcohol was discovered in England. It put cheap gin within the reach of the poorest people, and a good part of the country went on "the worst binge in history." Between 1690 and 1721 the number of gallons of spirits on which tax was paid rose from forty-three thousand a year to two million, eight hundred thousand. Thousands of drunks roamed England, and mass alcoholism caused a frightening rise in disease and death.

The health consequences were so great and widespread that the Royal College of Physicians appointed a committee of doctors who "had observed with concern for some years the fatal effects of several sorts of distilled spirits upon great numbers of both sexes; rendering them diseased, not fit for business, poor—and too often the causes of weak, feeble, and distempered children, who must be instead of an advantage and strength, a charge to the Country."

The Royal College petitioned Parliament to act. This led to a great political fight. The Whig party held power through favoring cheap gin, but there were other economic forces at work—the growers and importers of tea. They lobbied effectively and forced Parliament to change the tax structure in favor of their product. People were taxed out of alcoholism, which is why the British became a nation of tea drinkers instead of gin guzzlers. A historian reports, "Chronic alcoholism declined, and changes in the dietary habits brought the death rate from gin addiction down."

One way to control smoking that is being considered in Sweden is to impose a very high tax, like the one in England on gin. Cigarettes currently cost $1.35 a pack in Sweden; the government plans to raise the price in steps to $3.25 a pack. Becoming conscious of the money cost does help a great many people cut down or turn off. According to California tax official Richard Nevins, the only significant drop in the state's cigarette consumption since the surgeon general's report of 1964 occurred in 1967 when California raised cigarette taxes from three cents to ten cents a pack.

To help you put the economic motive to work for you, we recommend that at this point you take an envelope— any envelope—and write or type on it the following: Cigarette Mad Money Envelope.

Instructions:

Calculate how much you spend for cigarettes per day, as follows:

A _____	Number of packs I smoke a day.
B × 30 _____	Multiplied by 30, to cover the next 30 days.
C _____ (total)	Total number of packs you would smoke during the next month.

D ____   Price per pack that you pay.

E × ____   Multiplied by the total number of packs (C) that you would smoke during the next 30 days.

F ____
(total)   Now, place this amount of money into the envelope. Buy only one pack at a time, and only with the money from this envelope. If you have a supply of cigarettes, buy them from yourself by taking the money from this envelope—but only one pack at a time.

  If you decide to quit smoking, seal the envelope with whatever money remains in it. And when the 30 days are up, take the money and buy yourself something with it.

One way that some people continue to stay off cigarettes is to tape to a calendar, daily, the amount of money they would normally spend for cigarettes. You might try this to help you with your resolution. No, you won't have to do it for the rest of your life or even the rest of the year. If you stay off for a month, you'll probably have it made.

Besides the personal savings from eliminating cigarettes, a variety of positive financial benefits are available to non-smokers. These rewards are part of a developing national trend, businessmen translating the proved deaths and disabilities caused by smoking cigarettes into profit and loss, and paying dollar bonuses or giving cash discounts and other incentives to those who don't smoke or who quit.

In 1965, Columbia University's Teacher's College studied the "Association between Smoking and [Auto] Accidents" among 1,025 men who applied for car insurance. Dividing them into three groups by the number of accidents and driver violations, the investigators found that of those with no accidents or violations only 17.3 percent were smokers, but in the group with the highest rate of accidents and traffic violations nearly half smoked. Columbia called the difference "statistically significant" and added that the kind of dependence associated with smoking was also associated with lack of responsibility, resulting in poor driving.

The Farmers Insurance Group of Los Angeles checked this by comparing the accident records of 3,390 nonsmoking men who held Farmers auto insurance with those of an equal number of smoking policyholders. The results were startling: smokers had had just about twice as many auto accidents as nonsmokers.

In March 1971, the company translated this information into special nonsmoking auto insurance sold experimentally in two states, Wisconsin and Washington. Qualifiers who signed a statement saying they hadn't smoked a cigarette in the past two years got a 20 percent discount, amounting to forty dollars off the average premium. The truth of the statements was checked through a credit agency.

Farmers Insurance compiled the accident statistics of six thousand people who qualified for the nonsmoking policy and matched them with the number of accidents of smokers who bought car insurance during the same period. The results were "so good I can't believe them," says their actuarial vice president, Parke Godwin. Nonsmokers had only about one-third to one-half as many accidents as smokers. The nonsmoker's auto policy discount is now available in twenty-two states. Godwin believes that smokers' poor accident records are due to taking eyes and mind off the road to light up at high speed, or being distracted by burning ashes in the car. Smoking also dims vision, particularly at night, reducing smokers' margin of safety on the highway.

The Hanover Insurance companies have come out with a nonsmokers' homeowners' policy with discounts ranging from 7.5 to 23 percent. It's available in New York, Massachusetts, and Georgia, and soon will be in Illinois, Indiana, and Wisconsin. Savings are calculated on the fact that 70 percent of all building fires are in residences, and of these, 40 percent of dollar losses come from fires caused by smoking and matches used in smoking. The premium discounts reflect the hard actuarial fact that a nonsmoking family is considerably safer, according to Hanover's president, John Adams, Jr.

In Arlington, Texas, a couple of years ago, Sherry Park Apartments began renting units for from $180 to $195 a month, unfurnished, but newly decorated with expensive draperies and wall-to-wall carpeting. Knowing from experience that fabrics were often ruined by cigarette burns and that smokers littered the grounds around the building with butts costly to pick up, the owners decided to offer a ten-dollar-a-month rent reduction to any tenant who signed a simple form stating, "No one living in our apartment smokes." Guests were exempted, no questions asked, all on the honor system. Within three months, 146 nonsmoking lessees were saving $1,460 a month. Later, three families confessed to having started smoking, and began shelling out an extra ten dollars a month each.

The discount paid off as calculated, according to Mrs. Anita Maxfield, the building's manager, who added that smokers are not only more of a fire hazard to the landlord but to themselves also. Statistics bear her out. Building fires caused by smoking kill about eighteen hundred Americans a year and burn up more than $100 million in property (see Appendix E).

In Bristol, Rhode Island, several years ago, Mrs. Marian Dahl read a letter in Ann Landers's column from a non-smoking secretary who asked why people like herself, who didn't cause wastebasket fires or take time out to smoke, and didn't use as much sick leave as their smoking co-workers, shouldn't be rewarded for their efficiency. Mrs. Dahl read the letter to her nonsmoking husband, George W. Dahl, head of a Bristol valve manufacturing company, and suggested that this might make sense for his employees.

Mr. Dahl was receptive. He had recently lost two valued employees who were his good friends, one to lung cancer and the other to emphysema. Both had been heavy cigarette smokers. Dahl worked out a Cigarette Quitter's Pledge which guaranteed any employee who gave up cigarettes entirely, and didn't smoke a pipe or cigars while at work, two dollars a week extra. Immediately, forty of the plant's seventy smokers signed the pledge and quit. They were on their honor to report backsliding. Dahl put out candy, carrots, and apples "to keep them from climbing the walls." The bonus worked so well that Dahl increased it to three dollars for people who would give up all forms of tobacco all the time.

The scheme currently costs Dahl about $7,500 annually. The company counts it worthwhile in morale and health benefits alone. But Mr. Dahl noted that the company does profit from less employee absenteeism due to illness and from increased efficiency—plus the fact that the windows don't need cleaning so often. Dahl, an engineer, explained that seventy people smoking steadily in a closed, air conditioned building cause a heavy smudge build-up on the glass. Now the windows are cleaner and so are the employees' lungs.

A number of other employers have offered shorter-term bonuses. One is Alex McClendon, ex-smoker and vice president of the Shrewsbury, New Jersey, plant of Ebasco Industries, a small conglomerate. In 1968, shocked by a *Reader's Digest* article, "What the Cigarette Commercials Don't Tell You," McClendon told his employees that if they stopped smoking for twelve months he would give each a Christmas bonus equal to ten dollars a month, or one hundred and twenty dollars. In December that year he paid out $3,960 to the thirty-three (of forty) employees who did not smoke during the year. McClendon figured that the company saved twice that amount in reduced sick leave and thirty additional working minutes per day per employee, formerly wasted in smoking.

Although the bonuses were given only once, almost all

the employees who stopped smoking have stayed off cigarettes, so, McClendon says, the company continued to benefit by about eight thousand dollars or so a year.

The largest and most impressive financial windfall for
nonsmokers is the discount offered on life insurance by
about a dozen companies. It's impressive because it says in
cold cash that nonsmokers live longer than smokers. And
it's huge, involving more than $2 billion worth of insurance.

In 1964, H. Ladd Plumley, then president of State Mutual of America, and a one-time heavy smoker, did some
figuring. Evidence had been accumulating that smoking
caused most lung cancer deaths as well as many deaths from
certain other diseases. Therefore, in insurance terms, a nonsmoker should be considered a "preferred risk" meriting
lower premiums, just as a fireproof building qualifies for
cheaper fire insurance. But life insurance companies base
rates on actuarial tables that must be approved by state
commissions, and until January 1964, facts were scarce.
Then the surgeon general of the U.S. Public Health Service
published his famous report on smoking and health. For
the first time there was authoritative medical and scientific
opinion that cigarettes were deadly to a huge number of
people. And the report also showed how and why. The key
fact for insurance companies was this: cigarette smokers
had an overall death rate 68 percent higher than nonsmokers.* The report also stated that stopping, or cutting
down on, cigarettes would "delay or avert a substantial portion of deaths."

Immediately, State Mutual began advertising that "the
noncigarette smoker, in our opinion, is a better life insurance risk. He's entitled to a better rate. So we've given it to
him." They began selling whole-life insurance in minimum
amounts of ten thousand dollars at a 3 percent discount to

---

* The death rate is usually the number of deaths per hundred thousand population. Thus, of every 268 deaths per hundred thousand, 168
were smokers, 100 nonsmokers.

all who would sign the statement, "I do not now smoke cigarettes nor have I smoked any cigarettes for at least the past twelve months." This would save a nonsmoking thirty-one-year-old man fifteen dollars a year on a ten-thousand-dollar policy. On larger amounts, savings are substantial. Recently, an executive bought three hundred thousand dollars of nonsmoking insurance because the premium was one thousand dollars a year cheaper than for the same amount of insurance from a company which offered no discount.

In the first year, the company wrote $41 million worth of the new policies, and business has been climbing. Through 1973, the company had sold more than $1.7 *billion* of nonsmoking insurance; today this accounts for 33 percent of their new business.

The nonsmoking policyholders are not only better risks, but they buy larger policies than smokers do, and hold on to them more consistently. Perhaps it's easier for them to pay premiums because the money they save on cigarettes helps carry their insurance. A thirty-year-old man can buy his fifteen-thousand-dollar policy with what he saves on a pack and a half of cigarettes per day.

The company uses the same checkup system as Farmers —a credit rating company. Almost all applicants have turned out to be honest. One man did try to outfox the company by smoking only at night, but a neighbor spotted him and told the investigator. A man who had never smoked nearly lost the discount because one of his disaffected employees told the credit people that the insured was a secret smoker.

Thus far, the number of deaths has been lower than expected, so State Mutual believes that nonsmokers' premiums will be even lower in the future. And they've added a nonsmoker's disability policy at a 5 percent discount.

Other life insurance companies have adopted the idea. Phoenix Mutual offers discounts to nonsmokers whose height–weight ratio falls within their scale. And ten other smaller companies have their own "no smokers."

Many people have unhooked themselves from cigarettes simply by working out their own personal economic incentive. W. J. Kortesmaki, fifty-seven, of St. Paul, Minnesota, a pack-and-a-half-a-day smoker, decided to quit cold in 1953. To keep himself honest, he began putting twenty cents a day, the 1953 price of a pack of cigarettes, in a fruit jar. Later he changed the coins for paper money.

In four years he had put aside $292, and he and his wife, Martha, both children of Finnish immigrants, started a savings account to finance a trip to Finland. As the years went by, Kortesmaki increased his daily deposits to keep pace with the rising price of cigarettes. In 1970 he had $2,882 in the account, including $437 in interest, enough to pay for a five-week European trip for himself, his wife, and their two teen-age daughters. Every penny was money he hadn't burned.

Other Americans have devised financial gimmicks to give up smoking:

—Two men who worked for the Matson Steamship Line in San Francisco bet each other a dollar a day they would not smoke, and kept increasing the bet by a dollar every day. They've been off cigarettes for three years now, and neither can afford to pay the other eleven hundred dollars to start again.

—A Chicago housewife stopped smoking and asked the American Cancer Society for a coin-collection card. Each day, she put a quarter in a slot instead of spending it on cigarettes. When the card was filled, she turned it in and started another . . . and another. She hasn't smoked in more than two years, and the society has an extra $190 to fight cancer.

—An Atlanta, Georgia, housewife bought a money order for $292, the amount she figured on spending in one year for two packs of cigarettes every day. She gave it to her husband, telling him that if she smoked within the year he was to cash it and keep the money. She stayed off cigarettes and used the money order to replenish her wardrobe.

—A high school teacher in Randolph, Massachusetts, persuaded three-quarters of the town's smokers to give up cigarettes for one day—and contribute the price of a pack of cigarettes each to the school scholarship fund. The teacher reported that the fund received thirty-five hundred dollars and that a Wisconsin town had contacted him to plan a similar "smoke out" to help American Indian orphans.

The first big-business man to put the smoking problem in terms of profit and loss for his business, and to do something about it in a businesslike way, was Arthur T. Roth, then chief executive of the huge Franklin National Bank, with ninety-eight branches on Long Island and in New York City. A nonsmoker, Roth had often warned his colleagues of the health dangers of cigarettes but had made little impression. Then, several years ago, shocked by the death from lung cancer of a valued vice president, a heavy smoker, he took a new tack. A careful study revealed that smoking employees were costing the bank seven dollars a week each in lower efficiency, greater absenteeism, and burned furniture and rugs. Since half the bank's twelve hundred employees smoked, Roth figured this was draining Franklin National of more than $100,000 a year, about 1.5 percent of its profit.

The directors had to heed a sum as large as this. They quit smoking at board meetings and the bank's officers gave up smoking at their desks. Then Roth could tell all employees "no smoking at work."

At first resentment was high and the ladies' and men's rooms were crowded with smokers. But within a couple of weeks the resentment vanished along with the smoke. In fact, many employees told Roth they were grateful for being forced to give up cigarettes during the day. Many were able to stop altogether. And a subsequent checkup showed that the original figures were correct—the bank's profits went up.

In 1969, when Congress was considering the Cigarette Labeling Act (since passed), Mr. Roth was invited to testify on what cigarettes cost the entire country. He came up with a total of about $9 billion a year. He estimated that it might be as high as $12 billion or more.*

Add to this the expense of illness and death due to cigarettes (more than $5 billion a year), and the actual retail cost of cigarettes, more than $11.5 billion in the most recent fiscal year, and you are well above $25 billion in cost.

Tobacco taxes totaled just over $5.5 billion in 1972–1973. The net national *expense,* therefore, comes to about $20 billion per year.

The toll of cigarettes in death, disease, suffering, and disability is well known. That's why there are nearly 30 million ex-smokers in this country today. Now that the costs are being figured in dollars and cents, and appropriate rewards are offered to individuals for quitting, many more may be inspired to stop burning up their money.

---

* Cost of higher fire insurance premiums, due
to smoking-caused building fires .... $0.2 billion
Cost of smoking-caused forest fires .... 0.1   "
Cost of higher prices of consumer goods
resulting from smoking-caused absenteeism,
etc. @ $4 per week per smoking worker
(lower than the bank figure) .... 8.0   "
Cost of higher life insurance premiums .... 0.6   "
Cost of higher health insurance premiums .... 0.5   "
Cost (uncalculated) in public cleanup, public
health, higher auto insurance, cigarette
damage to public buildings .... ?

Total .... $9.4 billion

Your Awareness

He [Sir Walter Raleigh] took a pipe of
tobacco a little before he went to the
scaffold, which some formal persons were
scandalized at, but I think 'twas well
done and properly done, to settle his
spirits.

> John Aubrey
> *Brief Lives II*

You've been wrapping and noting your reasons for smoking
your cigarettes for five days now. How about it? Have you
found that it makes you aware of the number of times you
smoke unconsciously? Has it become clearer to you that
you've taught yourself to become a smoker—and that you
can teach yourself to become the nonsmoker you used to be?

A. Review and summarize your reasons for wanting to
stop smoking.

B. Continue wrapping your cigarettes and keep a detailed
record of each one you smoke.

C. Never carry matches or a lighter.

D. Don't carry cigarettes. At home, put them in some dis-
tant spot like the basement, attic, or mailbox. At work, give
them to your secretary or coworker, or place them in the
back of a file drawer or behind a bookcase in another room.
But never have your wrapped pack within easy reach.

E. Start cutting down on the number of cigarettes you smoke by: (1) Making a pledge each morning of the number of cigarettes you are going to smoke that day. Note this on a card or a calendar. Each night before you go to bed check how close you came to your goal for the day. (2) Reducing the number of cigarettes each day in a way that seems best for you. Some people find that eliminating the cigarettes that count as number one (the most important—would have missed it very much) is the best way to start. Knocking out the most desired smokes makes it easy for some people to manage the rest. For others, getting rid of the least important (rated 4 and 5 on your list) works better.

No matter how you do it, try to smoke fewer cigarettes day by day; if possible, fewer each day than the day before.

Some people manage this better by starting to smoke thirty minutes later each day.

DAY TEN | *Action*

Your Personal World

Tobacco has been my evening comfort and
my morning curse for these five years.

> Charles Lamb
> Letter to Wordsworth

Up to this point you have checked yourself on three of the
four sets of key factors identified by research as involved
with giving up smoking. One is the psychological use of
smoking in your life; another is your perception of the
health threat and other hazards and costs of smoking; a
third is your personal values and your desire to change your
smoking habits. Today you are going to test the social factors in your life that generally reinforce smoking. It is still
a socially acceptable act, restricted only in such public
places as transport facilities, schools, and in certain industries such as oil refineries where an open flame is dangerous.
Only lately have several local and state laws been passed to
restrict smoking in more public places: restaurants, hospitals, beauty parlors, food shops, and doctors' offices.

It is considered hospitable to put out cigarettes for guests,
to offer a cigarette at a party. Matches and ashtrays are
ubiquitous, unspoken invitations to smoke.

An active and widespread reinforcer of the smoking habit is public smoking by well-known sports, entertainment, political, and other figures, especially on television and in motion pictures. Advertising is another very strong smoking reinforcer. It was most effective in commercials on television. But it cultivated its own contradiction when the Federal Communications Commission, after a successful lawsuit by ASH (Action on Smoking and Health) in 1967, enforced the "fairness doctrine," instructing TV and radio broadcasters to carry one free antismoking spot for every four paid cigarette commercial announcements. Even at the low ratio of one to four, these antismoking messages, using the same techniques as the cigarette commercials, are credited with being the biggest single factor in forcing down both total and per capita sales of cigarettes for the first time in more than ninety years. But when the "Public Health Cigarette Smoking Act" became law in January 1971, cigarette commercials were ruled out of broadcasting. And since then the number of antismoking spots has dropped off, and cigarette sales have been rising once more.

Besides, the $210 million formerly spent on TV and radio cigarette commercials became available for other kinds of advertising. The number of pages of paid cigarette promotion in national magazines, newspapers, and other media went up sharply.

Almost all of the social factors aid smoking and make quitting more difficult. Hence, anyone considering giving up cigarettes had best be aware of this problem and be prepared to counteract it. To aid you, we include the following self-test:

Does the World Around You Make it Easier, or Harder, to Change Your Smoking Habits?

Indicate whether you feel the following statements are true or false by circling the appropriate numbers. IMPORTANT: Answer Every Question.

	TRUE OR MOSTLY TRUE	FALSE OR MOSTLY FALSE
A. Doctors have decreased or stopped their smoking of cigarettes in the past ten years.	2	1
B. In recent years there seem to be more rules about where you are allowed to smoke.	2	1
C. Cigarette advertising makes smoking appear attractive to me.	1	2
D. Schools are trying to discourage children from smoking.	2	1
E. Doctors are trying to get their patients to stop smoking.	2	1
F. Someone has recently tried to persuade me to cut down or quit smoking cigarettes.	2	1
G. The constant repetition of cigarette advertising makes it hard for me to quit smoking.	1	2
H. Both government and private health organizations are actively trying to discourage people from smoking.	2	1
I. A doctor has talked to me at least once about my smoking.	2	1
J. It seems as though an increasing number of people object to having someone smoke near them.	2	1
K. Some cigarette advertisements remind me to smoke.	1	2
L. Congressmen and other legislators are showing concern with smoking and health.	2	1

M. (NOTE: This question cannot be used as specifically as the others.) The people around you, particularly those who are close to you (e.g., relatives, friends, office associates), may make it easier or more difficult for you to give up smoking by what they say or do. What about these people? Would you say that they make giving up smoking or staying off cigarettes more difficult for you than it would be otherwise? (Circle the number to the left of the statement that best describes your situation.)

3 They make it much more difficult than it would be otherwise.
4 They make it somewhat more difficult than it would be otherwise.
5 They make it somewhat easier than it would be otherwise.
6 They make it much easier than it would be otherwise.

How to Score Yourself:

1. Enter the numbers you have circled on the test questions in the space below, putting the number you have circled to Question A over line A, to Question B over line B, etc.

2. Total the three scores across on each line to find your totals. For example, the sum of your scores over lines A, E, and I gives you your score on Doctors; lines B, F, and J give the score on General Climate, etc.

				Totals
A	E	I	=	Doctors
B	F	J	=	General Climate
C	G	K	=	Advertising Influence
D	H	L	=	Key Group Influences
		M	=	Interpersonal Influences

Scores can vary from three to six. Six is high; five, high middle; four, low middle; three, low. Learn below what your scores mean.

This test is somewhat of a preview of what may happen

when you try to quit smoking. Besides the strong pull of the habit and its links with your life, and whatever physical craving you may have for nicotine, you will either be aided or dissuaded from your attempt by the world around you.

Surveys have identified the five factors in the smokers' world, checked in the above test, that are of most importance. If you score low on a factor, it may work against you; if you score high, it can be of real help.

Doctors. For most people, their doctor's opinion of health problems has a strong influence on their attitudes. And your doctor, if he is part of the vast majority of the medical profession that sees smoking as harmful to health, can assist you in getting off or staying off cigarettes. The fact is that more than half the United States doctors who formerly smoked cigarettes have quit, and nearly all doctors believe that it is their duty to warn their patients not to smoke. If you score five or six in this factor, talk to your doctor about smoking and take his advice.

General Climate. As you have been a smoker, chances are your environment has been congenial to your habit. If this is so, you will score low in this factor, and it will be a very good idea for you to change your environment as much as possible while you're trying to kick the habit. Seek out the company of nonsmokers or of others like yourself who are trying to stop, or of those who have succeeded in giving up cigarettes. As much as possible, stay away from places where smoking is permitted and try to frequent places where smoking is discouraged if not prohibited; not permanently, just while you're quitting.

Advertising Influence. If you score low in this category, you are strongly influenced by cigarette advertising. Again, the thing to do is, as much as possible, avoid exposing yourself to this reinforcer of your habit. This is not as difficult as it used to be when there were TV commercials, but there is still much cigarette advertising in newspapers, on billboards, and in many magazines. To combat this advertising you might try a mental trick: when you do see an advertisement promoting the notion that cigarettes are glamorous or masculine or seductive, try to reverse the message by using some of the information you have read in previous chapters.

Key Group Influences. All of us are influenced to some extent by certain key groups in our lives. If you score high here, you are aware of and influenced by the actions of the federal government, public and private health agencies, and schools. All are on record that smoking is harmful, and all are actively engaged in programs to reduce cigarette smoking. On the other hand, a low score does not mean that you are not susceptible to some other influences which may have the same purpose as these, perhaps a church group or civic organization or a sports team. Try to maximize the contact and influence of those that can support you in your desire to stop smoking.

Interpersonal Influences. Most of us are sensitive to certain individuals. The strongest influences may vary; for some, it may be wife or husband; for others, the children, or parents, or the people at work. Because there are so many personal influences, it isn't possible to be entirely specific with this question. But if your answer to M scores five or six, the people who are important to you are likely to be supportive of your desire and effort to quit smoking.

—A young New Jersey widow found that her six-year-old son was hiding her cigarettes. When she punished him, he told her tearfully, "Mommy, I don't want you to die, too." Shocked, the woman realized that what seemed to her a pleasurable habit was frightening the child, and this helped her decide to quit smoking.

—The wife of a California automobile mechanic said to her husband, "Smoking smells up the house, and it's a bad example for the children." He could continue to smoke if he wanted to—but he'd have to do it outside. A spell of rainy weather made it easy for him to give up cigarettes.

DAY ELEVEN

O metaphysical tobacco
Fetched as far as from Morocco,
   Thy Searching fume
   Exhales the Rheum
O metaphysical tobacco.

Anonymous

This is the second Day devoted to reading and contemplation leading, like Day One, to further Action. This Day, please read the next five chapters to gain the following information to help you quit:
1. Strategies that work best for the type of smoker you are.
2. Proof, in two detailed personal stories, that quitting is indeed a process.
3. An alternative course: nonprofessional group therapy for those who choose to quit in company.
4. Is it really necessary to stop smoking? Couldn't you just switch to cigars or a pipe?
5. Practical answers to the twenty questions about giving up the habit most frequently asked of doctors by apprehensive smokers.

1. Kind of Smoker + Motivation + Technique = Quitting

The scatterbrain, Tobacco. Yet a man of
no conversation should smokc.

> Ralph Waldo Emerson
> *Journals* (1866)

In order to quit it is important to know, as you now do,
what kind of smoker you are and what your motives are for
giving up smoking. But there is one more step, the actual
process of quitting. There are various ways to go about this,
and some work better with one type of smoker than with
another. So, before you try quitting, guide yourself by the
following information in selecting your method.

Stimulation

If you smoke for this reason, you belong with about 10
percent of the smoking population. Smoking wakes you up,
organizes your cnérgies, and keeps you going.

To quit, you must find a safe substitute, another source
of stimulation. A young executive was smoking four packs

a day when he met his wife-to-be. She, a nonsmoker, let him know that she would be happier if he didn't smoke. The idea appalled him. "What'll I do when I want a cigarette?" he asked. "Take a deep breath," she replied.

He tried it, and in four hours he was off cigarettes. It was just as easy as that, he insists, and the record bears him out. From four packs a day to zero in four hours—and he hasn't smoked in six years.

Other things that help the stimulation smoker to turn off cigarettes are a brisk walk, moderate exercise (with your doctor's permission), chewing gum, or a new hobby. In a West Coast smoking group, the quitters were advised to take a drink whenever they felt a desire to smoke. One member went on a three-day binge but came back to report proudly, "I never had a single cigarette."

Try getting up earlier in the morning and you won't need a cigarette to give you that quick pickup.

Handling

Handlers represent another 10 percent of smokers. If you're one, you like to keep your hands busy. You enjoy playing with a cigarette and blowing smoke. You enjoy lighting up, have your own way of holding a cigarette.

To help yourself quit, find something else that is satisfying to manipulate. A plastic cigarette may help. Worry beads will keep your fingers busy. Try doodling or even drawing—keep a notebook handy. Finger a coin in your pocket, or, like Captain Queeg, some ball bearings. Carry a pocketknife and a piece of wood for whittling, or have knitting needles and wool with you.

Warning: Often this type of smoker will try smoking a pipe or cigar, or carrying an unlit cigarette as a substitute. This can work, but it's chancy. Usually these people go back to cigarettes. It's much better to find a substitute without the sight, smell, or taste of tobacco.

Relaxation

Fifteen percent of smokers smoke when relaxed. Thus, a cigarette is a kind of present to oneself, a reward for a job well done. It enhances the pleasure of some already pleasurable situation like eating or making love. It is a bonus for solving some problem or overcoming an obstacle.

If you're like this, then you have to decide whether the cigarette really gives you pleasure, whether you smoke it to preserve something good and not let it turn sour, or to avoid feeling bad, in other words.

If you really enjoy smoking and regard it as a reward, it will be very easy for you to find a substitute, or several substitutes, and to give up cigarettes. Just do more things that please you, and consider the ill effects of smoking. People like you never seriously miss cigarettes.

Stimulation-Handling-Relaxation

The above three categories of smokers, which together account for about 35 percent of the smoking population, have three things in common:

1. They are all involved with good, positive feelings; the smoker uses cigarettes to enhance his pleasures.

2. To quit, these kinds of smokers need an adequate substitute.

3. And for these smokers, quitting is not difficult.

Crutch or Stress

About 30 percent of smokers use cigarettes as something to lean on in moments of stress, discomfort, or pressure. According to Dr. Hans Selye, "Life in an advanced technological society . . . exposes the individual to a barrage of excessive stimulation" or stress, which often amounts to an assault on the spirit. Our bodies are programed to react to stress as our primitive ancestors did when threatened with danger—blood pressure increases, digestion stops, and a number of other physical reactions take place which are designed to help us fight or run away.

We react this way automatically (this part of our nervous system is largely out of our control) and in order to short-circuit stress and find peace and tranquility, most of us take up what Dr. Selye calls "diversional activity." This includes everything from foot tapping or chewing on a pencil to drug and alcohol addiction.

Smoking is a diversional activity, says Selye. "The choice is not 'to smoke or not to smoke,' but whether to smoke or to overeat, to drink, or merely to fret and bite our fingernails."

Thus, the stress smoker lights up when tense, angry, frustrated, or when he anticipates trouble. To quit requires deliberately facing such situations without a cigarette. A Sausalito, California, housewife said that she could never enter a roomful of strangers except behind her own personal smoke screen. When she found out that she was a stress smoker, she deliberately attended a party where she had few friends and left her cigarettes at home. "I walked in not smoking and—no problem," she reported later quite happily. Such people can be aided by the substitutes we mentioned earlier—physical activity, eating, drinking, and so on—but the key to quitting is managing stress without smoke. It seems frightening in prospect; but in retrospect it usually isn't all that bad.

Need or Craving

About 25 percent of smokers may be described as psychological addicts in their dependence on cigarettes. They begin to crave the next cigarette the moment they've extinguished the one they're smoking. They're constantly aware that something is missing when they're not smoking. They feel hooked and are usually terrified at the prospect of being without cigarettes for an extended period of time.

This type of smoker has to quit all at once. One way to help the process is to smoke a great deal more than usual for a few days. This spoils the taste and makes it easier to stop. Or wait for your next bad cold when cigarettes lose their taste and you don't really want to smoke. You must isolate yourself from cigarettes completely until the craving is gone. The worst period is the first fifteen days.

A person who needs to smoke is more likely to have nervous reactions, but these can be managed. (See Day Eleven, Section 5, for practical advice on what to do when you quit smoking.) In one way, the very difficulty of getting off cigarettes is an advantage for this smoker. Once he's managed to quit, he's more likely to quit permanently. He just doesn't want to go through the experience another time.

Reflex

This type of smoker, who makes up about 10 percent of the smoking population, lights up almost unconsciously and gets little or no satisfaction from his cigarettes.

The biggest help toward quitting is becoming aware of smoking, and the wrap sheet does this very effectively.

The successful reflex quitter must be aware of, and interrupt, the reaction that leads from a cup of coffee or a drink or a snack to a cigarette. Cigarettes have to be kept out of sight and out of reach.

A New York City saleswoman did most of her smoking at night, partly out of loneliness. In order to break the pattern, she locked her cigarettes in the mailbox of her apartment building, which was in the lobby. She lived on the thirtieth floor. She could smoke whenever she wanted to, but she had to leave her apartment, take the elevator, open her mailbox—and she forced herself to smoke only in the lobby. It all seemed too much trouble for the amount of pleasure she got out of it. Cutting out her smoking at night made it comparatively easy to quit during the day, since she was not permitted to smoke on the job.

If this kind of smoker really feels the need of a cigarette, a useful trick is to look into a mirror and ask, "Do I really want to smoke?"

The Craving-Crutch-Reflex smokers use cigarettes to modulate their feelings so that they will feel better. For them, substitutions don't work. They learn to quit by managing the situations which produce bad vibrations without a cigarette.

2. Quitting Is a Process

I have seen your dispatch expressing your unwillingness to break your hold where you are. Neither am I willing. Hold on with bull-dog grip, and chew and choke as much as possible.

> Abraham Lincoln, Telegram to General Grant as Grant settled down for his long siege of Petersburg (17 Aug., 1864)

Probably the biggest misconception about giving up cigarettes is that it must always occur all at once and continue permanently to be successful. But, as we've mentioned, surveys show that it doesn't usually happen that way. As we've seen, some people can cut from four packs a day to zero and stay off cigarettes, but this is not the usual pattern.

The wife of psychologist J. D. Nolan was a pack-and-a-half-a-day smoker who wanted desperately to quit but couldn't. Finally, six years ago, she asked her husband for professional advice. He started by telling her to confine her smoking to a single place, a "smoking chair," which was positioned so that she could not watch television or carry on a conversation. While she was in that chair, nobody in the house was supposed to speak to her, and she was instructed not to read. She had to keep a record of what she smoked.

Within a couple of days, Mrs. Nolan had cut her consumption to less than half, twelve cigarettes a day. But that was as low as she could go, so her husband moved the chair to the cellar. Smoking only in the cellar, she cut down to five cigarettes a day. She got bored with recording her cigarettes and stopped doing so, but otherwise continued to smoke only in the cellar. Her smoking went up to seven cigarettes a day.

In other words, when smoking was isolated from the usual satisfactions in the environment, it became considerably less pleasurable, proof that the environment is a strong reinforcer of the habit. But there was still enough of a residue of gratification to support a seven-cigarette-a-day habit. However, after two weeks at this level, Mrs. Nolan told her husband that "she was disgusted with her inability to quit smoking and she was disappointed with the self-control program." The following day she stopped smoking completely, and when last heard from was still off cigarettes. As the professionals describe it, "Apparently, standard conditioning techniques weakened the habit behavior to the point where it could be 'voluntarily' controlled."

This woman had professional advice in cutting down, but aside from that and the cooperation of her family, she was able to kick the habit finally without any special treatment. What she did was to disrupt her smoking environment, and any smoker can work out a similar plan.

The famous educator Dr. S. I. Hayakawa says that he was "the average steady smoker—twenty to thirty cigarettes a day—for thirty years or more. I had a cigarette on waking, smoked while driving, after each lecture, and during seminars."

Then he began to dislike smoking and wanted to quit, which he did "like Mark Twain, dozens of times. None lasted more than a few days."

Although not himself a psychiatrist, he was invited to be a visiting lecturer at the famous Menninger School of Psychiatry, in Topeka, Kansas. By this time his smoking had become "so compulsive that I was breaking my cigarettes in half, not to cut down, but to double their impact by lighting up forty times to a pack. I never used filters."

Dr. Hayakawa says he knew that "will power was of no help in my smoking problem. . . . I decided not to try to stop [but to study] carefully everything about my smoking— when I smoked, how much I enjoyed it, under what conditions I increased my smoking." (You will notice that he did what the wrap sheet has done for you.) "I decided, too, to notice the effects on my surroundings—the smell of my clothes and the curtains, the dirty ashtrays. . . .

"I started taking notes. Out of a package of twenty, how many had I actually enjoyed? The answer varied from day to day, but it was a rare day when I could say I enjoyed three —and of these only the first two or three puffs. I took notes on the accumulation of phlegm in my throat, on the awful taste in my mouth in the morning, I stared at the yellow on my fingers. But I made no attempt to cut down or quit. . . . My only rule was not to smoke unconsciously or automatically.

"After six weeks, I found myself continuing to smoke heavily but becoming more miserable about it. At this point I underwent a curious self-concept change, from 'I am a smoker' to 'I am a nonsmoker.' Despite my continued smoking, I was convinced of my new self-concept, 'I am a non- smoker, in spite of a temporary thirty-year addiction.' I know this sounds ridiculous, but that's the way it was.

"After that happened, I knew it was only a matter of time before the addiction would disappear. Each morning I would ask myself, 'Do I want a cigarette?' Each morning I would say, 'Yes,' and light up. That first cigarette of the day was the key event. It meant I would continue smoking the rest of the day.

"Now I was more miserable than ever. I was not only not enjoying it and actively hating the taste and smell of the stuff, but I was in violation of my self-concept. It couldn't go on that way.

"And it didn't. In another six weeks my visiting professorship had expired and I was driving home to San Francisco. On the second day on the road I woke up in the morning and asked myself the usual question, 'Do I want a cigarette?' To my surprise the answer came out, 'No!' And I didn't need one the rest of the day, nor the next day, nor the next—nor any day since.

"All this happened in 1961. My cigarette addiction was completely out of my system. Not even a passing temptation to smoke has ever crossed my mind in the ensuing years.

"My self-treatment took three months. Yours may take more time—or less. Will power won't do it, unless you have a lot more of it than I have."

These two true stories about people who quit illustrate many of the principles we've been talking about and how to apply them. They are not the only strategies (there are many more, as you will see in Day Thirteen, Section 1) and perhaps you will invent your own, because the basic message of this book is just this: everything about smoking is personal. You started for your own reasons. You continued for your own motives. You want to quit because you've decided to do so for yourself. And you're going to do it in your own way and in your own time.

Remember, *there are no failures*. If you don't stop smoking it's because your desire to smoke is stronger than your desire not to smoke. There's nothing shameful about this. But it's not a life sentence. The fact that you are reading this indicates that you want to kick the habit and that you will probably do so sooner or later.

And continue to remind yourself that you haven't failed if you do stop—for a day, a week, a month, whatever—and then start to smoke again. This, too, is part of a normal process that many, probably most, people go through before they become nonsmokers. The fact that you were able to quit once, no matter for how short or long a period, indicates that you can do it again. And that eventually it will work. When you want it to.

Dr. William A. Hunt, professor of psychology of Loyola University in Chicago, writes that "the universal use of complete abstinence as the sole criterion of success in habit modification deprives the subject of the reinforcement value of partial success and unnecessarily damns him as a lost soul after one slip either of conscious indulgence or unconscious habit. After years of heavy cigar smoking I now regard myself as a nonsmoker, yet occasionally do indulge, perhaps on an average of once every six weeks. The reasons are immaterial . . . the important point is that such incidents are always greeted by colleagues with 'So you can't give it up,' 'Once a smoker, always a smoker,' 'Well, you're back on the habit'—remarks not calculated to reinforce a pattern of abstinence. Moreover, a certain anxiety and self-doubt usually intrude themselves into my thinking at such times, and it is necessary for me to remind myself that without errors there can be no learning curve."

3. If You Don't Want to Go It Alone

A cigarette is the perfect type of a
pleasure. It is exquisite and it leaves one
satisfied. What more can one want?

> Oscar Wilde
> *The Picture of Dorian Gray*

Much of the health information which has motivated many
Americans to want to stop smoking has been distributed
through the large public health agencies like the American
Cancer Society, the American Heart Association, and the
American Lung Association. But motivation has not proved
to be enough, as we have seen.

Many smokers want to quit but need help. For that reason, the American Cancer Society has felt responsible to go
the extra step and devise a simple method of assistance
which can be duplicated anywhere without professional help
or investment.

Their solution is a do-it-yourself group effort, most useful
for smokers who don't want to make the cessation effort by
themselves. It succeeds with about 60 percent of those who
try it. That is, about 35 percent quit cigarettes altogether

and the rest cut their smoking by at least one-half. Both results are desirable, since it's now known that cutting down is usually the first step toward quitting; and, besides, all smoking damage is dose related to the number of cigarettes, number of years of smoking, tar and nicotine content, and depth of inhalation.

The society's new project, initiated in July 1970 in twenty California communities, has been successfully tested on some 12,500 people in that state and thousands more in a dozen others.

All that the ACS method requires is a place to meet and an ex-smoker willing to spend two hours twice a week for four weeks to help a group of eight to eighteen smokers work out their problem. The group "facilitator"—deliberately not called "leader"—may also be a couple. Groups have been successfully conducted by engineers, housewives, and even high school students.

The best place to meet is a hospital, because it's open at night (most male smokers can only attend after work) and has parking facilities and meeting rooms equipped to show films and slides, plus a staff of professionals to call on for health information. But groups have worked well in offices, such as TRW, and Hughes Aircraft in Los Angeles, and in schools, churches, and libraries.

The people who were helped range from hard-core eighty-cigarette-a-day burners to four-cigarette-a-day neophytes, from a seventy-seven-year-old man who'd smoked for more than sixty years to a twelve-year-old girl just starting. Most groups are free, though some charge a small fee to hire a hall or pay a facilitator if they can't find a volunteer. The Kaiser Permanente Medical Care Program, affiliated with the ACS plan, charges fifteen dollars to those of its six hundred thousand members who need clinic help and twenty-five dollars to nonmembers. Some experts believe that a registration fee helps discourage doubtful members and keeps the others coming to meetings. Some think it useful to charge a dollar or two for each meeting. But even when fees are charged, those who can't afford to pay are made welcome.

"The biggest step toward quitting is just showing up at a group," says George M. Saunders, public health expert of the ACS California Division in San Francisco, who created the plan out of the experience of Dr. Fredrickson, several educators, and hundreds of ex-smokers. Saunders believes that for 52 million cigarette smokers there had to be 52 million reasons for starting and there will have to be 52 million reasons for quitting. But many need a group to elucidate their motives and keep them on the track.

James (only first names are used in groups) is a sixty-eight-year-old Napa businessman whose wife had forced him to smoke in the garage. "It got very lonely out there," he told his group. A thirty-five-year-old Berkeley mother, trying to kick her pack-a-day habit, brought her twelve-year-old daughter, who smoked only three or four cigarettes a day, to a group in Oakland. Both quit. A seventeen-year-old Oakland boy (a pack a day) brought his thirty-eight-year-old mother (forty cigarettes). They quit, too.

One of the first groups started because of the January 1971 California earthquake. The tremor stopped the elevators in a ten-story building in Los Angeles. Employees had to climb stairs to get to work, and many smokers couldn't make it above the third floor. The company decided to put in a quit-smoking clinic.

California has a state law that any child caught smoking or carrying smoking materials on school property must be disciplined. Dean of Students Joseph Rancatore at Ygnacio Valley High School thought mandatory suspensions wasteful. Instead, he gave students options: first offense, three thirty-five-minute after-school work details or a one-day suspension; second offense, a two-day suspension or join a smoking group.

The first Ygnacio group was run by a young mother who

had quit smoking in an ACS clinic. Group members were half a dozen sixteen-year-old sophomores who averaged about ten cigarettes a day. They all quit smoking after four weeks and volunteered to counsel other students.

Now, any Ygnacio Valley student up for smoking discipline can attend a four-week clinic with one of these teenage ex-smokers. When I visited the school, seven boys and girls were counseling twenty of their classmates in groups of two to four after school. Said Kathy Kirkland, sixteen, "It helps us ex-smokers stay off cigarettes, too."

Every facilitator must be an ex-smoker, for people wrestling with quitting do not believe that a person who has never smoked can comprehend their problem. Group members come in for the first time wary of being lectured on health and being forced to quit. They are relieved to learn that neither of these things happen. They are advised to go on smoking but not during actual sessions. There's a ten-minute break between the two hourly periods during which they can smoke, and they're assured that they can always go out for a smoke if they need one.

"A lot come in with a chip on their shoulder," says Marie Lenz, a fortyish housewife who has conducted successful clinics in Concord, California. "They say 'My doctor or my kids made me come. But I *know* I can't quit.' "

Groups help smokers identify their hangups and give practical help to deal with them. A stress smoker may stop and then, when the old pressures mount, may start smoking again. Knowing this in advance keeps him from feeling frustrated. Janet, a middle-aged group facilitator in the San Francisco Bay area who quit two years ago, was suddenly faced with a shocking death in her family and the loss of her husband's job. She began smoking, but when I saw her she said, "I know I'll quit again as soon as things simmer down."

To help members get to know one another and provide future support, many groups urge the buddy system. Members are asked to converse generally until they find a partner with whom they feel they can talk comfortably. Having a buddy helps quitters handle the "withdrawal symptoms" that afflict some. These are usually gone in two weeks, but can be frightening for someone who has to face them alone.

At the Kaiser Permanente Medical Center in Oakland, facilitators give out "Smokers' Survival Kits"—paper sacks filled with such things as sugarless mints, a hospital straw which can be bent into many shapes, special toothpicks, chewing gum, and other simple tranquilizers to help quitters over the rough spots.

Group sessions are enlivened by film showings, guest lectures, and anything to keep them interesting. But the main attraction is the group itself. Says Jim Henderson of the Martinez Health Department, "It's a kind of family. It reassures members they aren't the only ones with the same problem; [it] gives them support. It helps them make a commitment and follow through; part of it is competitive, part of it seeking approval. But the big result is realizing that the group helped itself—the facilitator only gets members involved, then they take over."

As the fourth session is ending, the facilitator suggests that now that the group has come to know one another and to recognize their motives, this might be a good time to try going without cigarettes. But only for the forty-eight hours just preceding the fifth meeting. If sessions are held on Monday and Wednesday at 8:00 P.M., the quitting trial starts on Saturday evening at 8:00 P.M.

The suggestion is not put on a make-or-break basis, and at the next session the facilitator doesn't quiz anyone about quitting. Almost all group members can manage two days without cigarettes, however. Those who can't, go on smoking and continue attending sessions. Actually, in many cases entire groups often give up smoking not just for forty-eight hours but right through the remaining four sessions, and a number of the members manage to stay off cigarettes after that.

"Helping Smokers Quit," a guide on how to start and run a group, is available free from any of the more than three thousand American Cancer Society offices in the United States (consult your telephone book) or from the national office, 219 East 42nd Street, New York, N.Y. 10017.

There may be a free "quit clinic" in your area. To find out, contact your local American Cancer Society or your local American Heart Association or National Lung Association. These three organizations often sponsor joint clinics. Your local county medical society may also know of a group. Besides these free clinics there are pay clinics such as Smoke-Watchers (five dollar registration, five dollars a session for fourteen sessions) and SmokEnders (sixty-five dollars for ten sessions) in some parts of the country, considered effective by those who need to make a financial commitment to support their quitting. The Seventh Day Adventists offer nondenominational five-day clinics.

4. Do I Really Have to Stop Smoking? Couldn't I Switch to Cigars or a Pipe?

A woman is a woman, but a good cigar is a Smoke.

Rudyard Kipling
"The Betrothed"

Many smokers ask these questions. The short, honest answer is that you *may* avoid *some* of the health hazards of cigarettes if you switch to cigars or a pipe.

The risk in smoking is mainly related to inhaling. Most people who smoke pipes and cigars do not inhale, because the smoke is too strong. A smoker has to inhale cigarettes to get his jolt of nicotine, but he can get the same effect by merely taking pipe or cigar smoke in his mouth. If he smokes this way, a pipe or cigars may be less hazardous— *not safer*—than cigarettes. However, nicotine affects blood circulation and the heart. In anyone who has circulatory or heart disease, the effect is about as bad whether the nicotine comes from cigars and pipes or from cigarettes. If the smoker switches to cigars and pipes and continues to inhale, he'll probably be worse off than before. And many cigarette smokers who switch to cigars and pipes do continue to inhale, probably increasing rather than decreasing their health hazard. Says Dr. Fredrickson, "In my experience heavy cigarette smokers who take up cigars or a pipe stay with these substitutes for a short period and then either stop completely or revert to cigarette smoking."

According to the 1973 report of the U.S. Public Health Service, "Pipe and cigar smokers in the United States [have] mortality rates slightly higher than those of nonsmokers, [Cigarette smokers' mortality rates are *much* higher.] The typical cigar smoker smokes fewer than five cigars a day, and the typical pipe smoker less than twenty pipefuls. Most report that they do not inhale. Those who do inhale infrequently and only slightly. As a result, the harmful effects appear to be largely limited to increased death rates from cancer at those sites exposed to the smoke."

Cigar smokers get as many mouth cancers as cigarette smokers, about one and one-half to four times as many as nonsmokers. Cancer of the larynx hits cigar, pipe, and cigarette smokers equally, too; about five times as often as it strikes nonsmokers. The same is true of cancer of the esophagus. In all these tumors, the rate goes up sharply when the smoker is also a heavy drinker of alcohol (more than seven ounces per day). One possible reason is that alcohol carries the noxious elements of tobacco smoke deeply into tissues. These relatively rare cancers account for 5 percent of male United States cancer deaths.

American cigar smokers die of lung cancer at about three times the rate for nonsmokers, pipe smokers at up to four times the rate, and cigarette smokers up to twenty-three times.

United States cigar and pipe smokers have at least a 55 percent greater risk of dying of emphysema than nonsmokers; for cigarette smokers the risk is 500 to 1,000 percent greater than the nonsmokers'. And cigar and pipe smokers have 150 percent to 300 percent more chance of dying of peptic ulcer than nonsmokers. Again, cigarette smokers have a much higher risk.

The difference is attributed to the difference in the amount smoked and in inhaling habits. "The death rates of current cigar smokers who said they inhaled at least slightly were appreciably higher than for men who never smoked regularly," reports statistician E. Cuyler Hammond of the American Cancer Society. Dr. Hammond's Cancer Prevention Study, which has followed more than one million Americans for six years, shows that people who say they inhale pipe or cigar smoke have the high death rate of cigarette smokers, and those who say they don't inhale reflect this in their longevity and health histories.

The National Clearinghouse for Smoking and Health points out that all smoking is dangerous; that noninhaling is relatively less hazardous than inhaling but not nearly so risk free as not smoking.

People who smoke certain brands of new little "light" filter-tipped cigars (twenty to a pack) are getting slightly less tar, and considerably less nicotine, per smoke than they would get from most popular brands of cigarettes. Too, the leading brand of little cigars, because of its "puffed" tobacco filter (which is to tobacco as Puffed Rice is to rice) gives only seven puffs of smoke as against ten from a king-sized cigarette. These two factors would probably reduce health hazards, because, as noted, all smoking danger is dose related. The assumption is, of course, that the smoker would not smoke more, and studies show that people who switch to milder brands do not usually increase consumption.

From this point of view, some little cigars might be preferable to some other brands of cigars or cigarettes. But most little cigars are within the range of cigarettes in tar and nicotine.

No matter what he smokes, the smoker should know the dangers of inhaling as well as the fact that risk increases with the amount smoked and the tar and nicotine content. He should not assume that just because the package says "Little Cigars," the product is less hazardous to smoke than a cigarette.

5. "Twenty Questions"

Tobacco, divine, rare, superexcellent tobacco,
which goes far beyond all the panaceas, pota-
ble gold and philosopher's stones, a sovereign
remedy to all diseases.

> Robert Burton
> *Anatomy of Melancholy*

Almost all smokers are apprehensive about giving up smoking. They have many questions—serious, disturbing questions—that prevent them from taking the final step. They
fear horrendous withdrawal symptoms. They can't face a
future bereft of cigarettes. They worry about putting on
weight.

Dr. Donald T. Fredrickson, Project Director of the Inter-
Society Commission for Heart Disease Resources, has
worked with many groups and individuals who needed help
in quitting. Out of his vast experience he has culled the
twenty questions most asked by would-be quitters. The
answers to these questions, below, are largely based on what
Dr. Fredrickson tells his patients.

Q. 1. Will I suffer "withdrawal" symptoms when I stop smoking?

A. Probably not. Many smokers experience few, if any, physical or psychological symptoms when giving up cigarettes. You don't have to program yourself for a period of horrible discomfort, based on misconceptions of how painful it's going to be. Knowing that stopping is not always arduous or unpleasant can be a strong psychological counterweight to what may have frightened you from quitting in the past.

Q. 2. What is the key period in quitting?

A. The first forty-eight hours. Once beyond this point, you are well on your way to becoming a nonsmoker. To help yourself through this period, prepare a three-day schedule filled with constant activity, leaving no time to sit around thinking about not having a cigarette. Remember, you're making the decision, and you can always decide to smoke again later if you wish.

Q. 3. How long will the craving or desire to smoke last?

A. Most people who quit, no matter how much they smoked or for what reason, report that the acute craving begins to subside after a few days. After two or three weeks there will be only an occasional desire—*not need*—to light up. It's important to keep this in mind, for many smokers give up on quitting because they say "I can't tolerate this intensive urge to smoke for the next couple of months, much less the rest of my life." Recognizing that the period of intense psychological discomfort is relatively short makes it much easier to accept it as a small price to pay for shedding a habit you really want to drop.

Q. 4. Why do I get so nervous when I try to stop smoking?

A. You know by now that cigarettes are used to modulate—control, enhance, suppress—feelings. When you stop smoking, both good and bad feelings must be managed without benefit of the cigarette, the lighting up, the inhaling, the whole act and sensation of smoking. This may result in a temporary build-up of tension and anxiety that feels like nervousness.

Q.   5.   If I do get symptoms, why, and how long will they last?

A.   These, too, are mostly the result of a sudden increase in tension. They are what doctors call "functional" and not organic symptoms, consisting as they do (nobody gets all of them) of nervousness, shortness of breath, tightness in the chest, heart palpitations, visual disturbances, sweats, abdominal discomfort, headaches, dizziness, fatigue, sleep disturbances, difficulty concentrating, and short temper. Look on these as signs that you are successfully adjusting to becoming a nonsmoker. Most subside within a matter of days or within a week. You may also cough more and bring up more sputum for a while. This only means that your lungs' cleansing mechanisms are no longer anesthetized and are beginning to sweep poisons from your body.

Q.   6.   Are any of these symptoms dangerous?

A.   No. If any symptoms should persist for more than two weeks, consult your doctor—they may be totally unrelated to smoking or quitting.

Q.   7.   Is there a safe number of cigarettes to smoke?

A.   No, not really, since each cigarette has an adverse effect on various parts of the body. There is some statistical support for thinking that smoking five cigarettes or fewer per day lowers the risk considerably, but, says Dr. Fredrickson, "I have yet to find a confirmed cigarette smoker (a pack or more a day) who has been able to bring it to this level and hold it for any period of time. In our experience nine out of ten will revert to their old smoking rates within weeks. As long as one continues to smoke, one adds fuel to a fire. The only way to extinguish the urge is to cut the fuel supply completely. Even then, it will take time for the residual desire to burn itself out."

Q.   8.   Is there a filter that makes smoking safe?

A.   No, but there are filters that reduce some of the hazards, mainly the risk of lung cancer. Not eliminate—reduce: a pack-a-day smoker has about twenty times the risk of cancer of a nonsmoker, but if he switches to a low-tar, efficiently filtered cigarette, his risk may drop to five times (500 percent) that of a nonsmoker. There are many chemicals in tobacco smoke that are not eliminated by filters.

Q.   9.   Are there any drugs my doctor can give me, or I can buy without a prescription, to help me?

A.   There are two general classes of drugs sometimes used to assist smokers in giving up cigarettes: 1) compounds, primarily lobeline, which simulate the taste sensations of smoking—spicy lozenges, silver nitrate preparations, and the like; and 2) drugs which modify symptoms or feelings associated with quitting—stimulants, tranquilizers, and sedatives.

        Some smokers report that antismoking preparations help them, but many scientfic studies do not bear this out. These differences may result from differences between people. You may try any nonprescription drug that helps you (sometimes doctors prescribe "placebos," or nearly inert drugs in impressive-looking forms). Dr. Fredrickson says, "To my knowledge, when taken according to instructions, none of the preparations available over the counter has short- or long-term harmful effects, nor any demonstrable addictive properties." Some doctors may prescribe a short course of a prescription tranquilizer, stimulant, or sedative to help a particularly nervous patient through the first few days without cigarettes.

Q. 10.   Can hypnosis help me quit smoking?

A.   Perhaps. There are some reports that hypnosis by a qualified psychiatrist or psychotherapist may aid some smokers. One doctor has made a film which demonstrates to doctors a technique for autosuggestion that he says has helped his patients. But hypnosis should be employed only by a truly qualified and responsible professional.

Q. 11.   Is cigarette smoking an addiction?

A.   The short answer is no. A more detailed answer would say that there is a pharmacological reaction to smoking, probably caused by nicotine, or else people wouldn't smoke. However, people do not become addicted as much to the nicotine as they do to all the surrounding habits, emotions, attitudes, and associations of smoking. Hence, "withdrawal" is more psychological than physiological. The key is *retraining*—creating a new set of habits. This requires three things: 1) Find a strong incentive to change. 2) Begin practicing nonsmoking by managing what were smoking situations without a cigarette. 3) Adopt a positive attitude toward being a nonsmoker that will reinforce the activity in that direction.

Q. 12.   What if I should smoke again?

A.   Just remember what you've learned: it's always your decision. So, if you should smoke again, that's what you decided to do—*you haven't failed.*

It's characteristic of relearning that one occasionally falls back into the old habit pattern. (Cf. Section 2, this Day, Eleven) Every day you stay away from cigarettes increases your chances of not going back, and every time you quit reinforces your ability to do so.

If you start smoking again, don't panic—and don't use it as an excuse that you just can't make it as a nonsmoker. This is the time when you are faced with another decision, that's all. You have to decide whether you really are a nonsmoker or want to become one, or are satisfied to remain a smoker. It's your choice.

Q. 13.   Will I notice immediate benefits if I quit?

A.   Yes. We've mentioned the rapid lowering of the

risk of heart attack and cancer. But more immediate is the sense of well-being reported by so many. One man quit when he found he couldn't play golf without leg cramps. After he stopped smoking, his leg cramps disappeared and he could easily play eighteen holes. Another had a constant, hacking cough, especially in the morning. It disappeared within two weeks after he quit cigarettes. A woman says, "I had sinus congestion, trouble sleeping, and I was constantly fatigued, suffered shortness of breath to the point where I couldn't go upstairs without feeling exhausted. When I stopped smoking most of my symptoms disappeared, and I really felt like a new woman. Even my complexion cleared up, and I look much younger."

Q. 14.   I had a grandfather who smoked all his life and lived to be ninety-five. How can you call it hazardous to health?

A.   Perhaps your grandfather didn't smoke very much and didn't inhale. Or maybe he was just lucky. Not every smoker dies young or gets lung cancer or a heart attack. Only the chances are so great—so much greater than for a nonsmoker—that it seems you are taking a very large risk for a comparatively small pleasure. Is it worth it?

Q. 15.   Isn't air pollution worse than smoking?

A.   From all information we have the answer is no. Even in jobs where the workers are exposed to known lung-damaging chemicals and mineral dusts, it's almost invariably only the smokers who get the serious lung diseases. Comparing people who live in smog-laden air, as in Los Angeles, with those who live in rural areas where the air is pure, again it's the smokers who turn up with the diseases—a smoking farmer suffers almost as much as a smoking city dweller (see Appendix D). As Dr. Fredrickson says, "Smoking cigarettes in a community with an air pollution problem simply compounds a felony." There seems to be a synergistic effect between polluted air and smoking.

Q. 16. If I quit smoking I'll crack up—or turn into an alcoholic.

A. Not likely. Once you've learned the technique of controlling and relearning one habit, you can do the same for others. Rather than becoming more self-indulgent without cigarettes, you'll be in much better control of yourself. You'll be able to handle problems better without smoking than you did with cigarettes. This is a fringe benefit of quitting.

Q. 17. You have to die of something—why not lung cancer?

A. It isn't only lung cancer—which is a lingering, horrible death—but smokers die *younger* on the average of a whole host of diseases, especially heart and circulatory diseases. They also develop crippling emphysema, with which they may live for years in a kind of half-world in which they are almost totally dedicated to inhaling enough oxygen. "As a physician," says Dr. Fredrickson, "I would submit that nothing is more tragic than the young person with fifteen or twenty years of life ahead who finds himself suddenly *crippled* with an irreversible chronic disease."

Q. 18. I think I'd rather take my chances of disease than suddenly get fat. How can I avoid gaining weight after quitting?

A. Again, you mustn't let misconception program you for obesity—it isn't inevitable for ex-smokers. Many people actually *lose* weight when they give up cigarettes. Some do have a strong drive to overeat. This may be partly a result of enjoying the taste and smell of food more. It may be caused by the change in body chemistry since the toxic effect of smoking has been removed. However, it is probably mainly a search for a sensual, oral cigarette substitute. If the ex-smoker lets himself go on an eating jag, he's only switching from one mood-modifying agent to another. He may need psychological or psychiatric support.

When a former smoker does gain weight, it's usually only a few pounds. This is a healthy, if temporary, trade-off. In order to equal the dangerous effects of smoking a pack a day, the ex-smoker would have to become eighty to ninety pounds overweight.

To avoid gaining weight, try these Actions:

—Buy a paperback calorie counter and figure out how much you are taking in in the way of weight gainers.

—Refuse second helpings.

—Eat more frequent small snacks, five or six a day, rather than loading up at three heavy meals.

—Watch your weight by stepping on a scale at the same time each day. This way you'll be warned to cut down on calories before you have an important weight problem.

—Drop high-calorie foods for low-calorie foods. No rich desserts (eat fruit instead), no butter on your bread or potato (fats are the most concentrated weight putter-oners). Use saccharine in your coffee; drink sugar-free soft drinks. Take a glass of wine rather than a cocktail, and cut way down on beer.

—Increase exercise, with your doctor's permission; it helps take your mind off smoking *and* burns some extra calories.

Q. 19. How about psychiatry, group therapy, and smoking clinics?

A. Says Dr. Fredrickson, "I believe only a small percentage of smokers will ultimately require the assistance of professional support. Most individuals are perfectly capable of stopping smoking on their own once they've made a *decision* to stop." However, many smokers find it easier to withdraw in a group (see Section 3, this Day, Eleven).

Q. 20. I've been smoking for many years. Isn't the damage already done?

A. Careful scientific studies show that no matter how long or how much you've been smoking cigarettes, when you stop, your body immediately begins to repair damaged cells and tissues. The numerous abnormal cells, which are probably precancerous, found in the lungs and throats of smokers, begin to change back to normal cells when the smoking stops. Unless there is true, irreversible disease, it is never too late to stop, and if there is chronic disease, stopping will help ensure that it won't get worse.

DAYS TWELVE THROUGH FOURTEEN

A branch of the sin
of drunkenness, tobacco
is the root of all sins.

James I of England
A Counterblaste to Tobacco

DAY TWELVE | *Action*

The 48-Hour Countdown

This very night I am going to leave off tobacco! Surely there must be some other world
in which this unconquerable purpose shall be
realized. The soul hath not her generous as-
pirings implanted in her in vain.

> Charles Lamb
> Letter to Thomas Manning

Review the questionnaires in reference to why you smoke
and how you feel about quitting. Can you put these together
with the smoking record you've been keeping and identify
the circumstances under which you are inclined to smoke
heavily—and which cigarettes are the most important to
you?

Continue trying to cut down on the number of cigarettes
you smoke in any way that seems most sensible and least
painful, or most manageable, to you (See Day Nine).

A. Review and continue all of the previous instructions.
B. Don't buy a fresh pack until you have finished your last
one. No reserves. Never buy a carton—only a pack at a
time. If you're afraid of going to bed or waking up without
a cigarette in the house, try to save the last one for these
emergencies.

C. Change brands twice during the coming week. Each time, move down to a lower tar and nicotine cigarette. This information is now printed on the package.

D. Select a two-day (48-hour) period when you think you'll be able to stop smoking.

If you think you can't do this without help, here are some suggestions for easing the trauma.

1. Reduce tension and nervousness by stepping up your physical activity, with your doctor's approval, in a way that won't strain your body. Walk at least half a mile or more each day. Make your motto "Never Ride When You Can Walk." This has been becoming easier as we have had periods of gasoline shortages.

2. Temporarily avoid activities you associate with smoking. If you smoke heavily while watching TV or having a drink, try not watching TV and stop using alcohol for a few days, only temporarily.

3. Stock up on interim cigarette substitutes. Make your own "Smoker's Survival Kit": chewing gum, flavored toothpicks (to chew on), and a plastic straw of the kind given to patients in hospitals. You can bend it, blow through it, and so forth. Dietetic candy and thin carrot and celery sticks are a help, too. Drink water, fruit juices, and low-calorie soft drinks; anything that keeps your hands and mouth busy when you want to smoke.

4. When you get the urge to smoke, try this breathing exercise: Sit down. Let yourself go completely limp—neck, arms, legs. Then take the deepest breath you can, inhaling slowly and fully. When you've taken in all the air you can comfortably hold, count to five. Then slowly exhale. Repeat this exercise several times.

5. Have a plan of action ready when temptation comes, a fall-back activity or series of activities. Use any of the above

ideas, plus any other tips you've read in this book (or will read—see **Day Thirteen**). Keep your hands busy. As suggested, a man can whittle or finger worry beads; a woman can knit. Carry a small cigarette holder or a fake cigarette you can handle and put in your mouth. Go visit a friend— *a nonsmoking friend.*

6. Many people who want to quit find it is easier to do so in company. Try to find another smoker who is willing to make the effort, someone you can talk to and feel comfortable with, whom you can compare notes with or call up when you need moral support. Or find someone who has quit who'll support you. This helps you over the rough spots.

7. Almost everyone who quits smoking works out some new gimmick or gadget for himself. But you may find that someone else's experience is helpful. So in the next chapter we give you the experiences of twenty-five former smokers who have quit.

Now you're ready for the dry run: *try quitting for just two days—only 48 hours—*during a time when it will be easiest for you. As we said, give yourself all the breaks. You can start today, or over the next weekend, or next week, or on your next vacation. But don't put it off too long or you'll never try.

You can carry an unopened pack of cigarettes during this trial if you wish. Some people like to have just one cigarette with them. In either case you'll know you can always change your mind.

Or, if you find temptation too strong when cigarettes are close at hand, you can try the other tack: hide ashtrays, lock up your cigarettes, and don't buy a new pack.

Experience shows that just about every smoker can manage 48 hours without cigarettes, and you have plenty of techniques in this chapter to help you through this period of no smoking.

I Did It My Way

Tobacco is a weed which is best left alone; it is not only a poison, but smoking of it may at any time cause a conflagration.

>   Kaibara Ekken
>   *Ten Kun*
>   (Ten Precepts of Health)

Today, while you are doing the first 24 hours of your 48-hour stint without cigarettes, is a Reading Day. You read this chapter consisting of many tactics, strategies, and gimmicks to bolster your 48-hour Action. And these techniques suggest a variety of Actions for you to take later on. All are practical, tested Actions that have helped someone, and some of them almost certainly will help you.

The real experts in quitting are those who have stopped smoking cigarettes. Here twenty-five different men and women, citizens of the United States and Canada, tell how they did it. They are real people, though their names are not given. These are their own words. One or two of their experiences are contradictory, but any reader will understand that this is because different types of smokers need to employ different strategies. Anything goes, as long as it's legal and it works for you.

—I made a rule that when I came home at night I could not smoke in my apartment. If I wanted to smoke, I had to go to the basement furnace room. This furnace room is always extremely hot. For the first couple of days I was dragging myself up and down the stairs several times a night. However, under no circumstances would I break the rule. Finally I gave up in disgust and stayed in my apartment one whole evening without smoking. It worked! I then developed a rule to make it awkward to smoke in another area of my daily routine. It worked again. Eventually I crowded the cigarettes out of my life altogether.

—I bought ten different kinds of cigarettes and placed one of each in my cigarette case. This meant every time I went to light up I had to smoke a different brand. This made smoking very unpleasant. It helped me to quit.

—When I went about my business without a cigarette on my person I would be tempted to buy a pack. However, if I carried *one* cigarette with me it provided a sense of security. I never "panicked" and was able to resist the temptation to smoke.

—I always *left open* the decision of whether or not to smoke. For example, if I were to say, "I won't have a cigarette now, but I *will* have one when I reach the office," invariably I would smoke a cigarette as soon as I arrived at the office. On the other hand, if I said to myself, "I won't have a cigarette now, postponing what I will do when I reach the office until I arrive," I found it much easier to control the urge to take the next cigarette.

—My experience in stopping smoking ten years ago was associated with a "craving" feeling located in my chest. I have, therefore, recommended on several occasions that people make a very "hot" (in the sense of "peppery") drink which they can carry around in a small Thermos bottle.

When they have an insatiable desire to smoke, they find that the curious sensation of having something "going down" in the upper chest is satisfied by drinking this mixture. It also gives them something to do with their hands and their mouth. Recipe: 1 quart tomato juice, ¾ cup lemon juice. Season to taste with several dashes each of Tabasco sauce, Worcestershire sauce, salt and pepper. The peppier the better! Shake well and serve hot or cold.

—Do what I did: tell all of your friends that you are going to stop smoking. This kind of public commitment really helped me to bolster my determination at those critical moments when I was tempted to weaken.

—Every day I would postpone taking the first cigarette by one half hour. In a short time I found I was able to make it to lunch without smoking. For me this was an absolute miracle, for I normally smoked at least a pack and a half during the morning hours. I stuck to my schedule, and to my surprise I soon found that I was not smoking at all.

—I smoked cigarettes for over forty-seven years. I did not start by smoking a pack a day; I worked up to it. If I wanted to quit smoking, I would have to work down to none a day. So I started my Count-Down System. I took a cigarette out of my package and put it in an empty pack. I did that every day for a week. The next week I took out two cigarettes each day. When the empty pack was filled, I smoked them. From then on it was a steady decrease . . . eighteen a day that week, seventeen the next week, and so on down to zero. Try my Count-Down Method IF you really want to quit cigarette smoking for good.

—One day I read in one of those doctor's columns that smoking was more of a nervous habit than anything—it was, most of all, *something to do with your hands.*

I kept thinking of what that doctor had said, that *the way to break a habit is to replace it with a good habit.* He gave some examples of what you could "do with your hands, and concentrate on," and the one I could best apply myself was knitting. I was no knitter, but I had learned how to do a "plain" and a "purl."

The first week was tough, the second tougher, but after that I was on my way to being a knitter instead of a smoker. After dinner, instead of picking up a cigarette, I picked up my knitting. When I went out in the car I took my knitting out of my purse. When I watched TV, I knitted. *Every time I wanted to reach for a cigarette, I reached for the knitting instead.* The first year I made a pile of squares, 304 three-and-a-half-inch nylon squares, in plain old garter stitch, to the accompaniment of the hockey games and plays, etc. on TV, and finally put them all together and turned them into a multicolored spread.

—I quit cigarettes and smoking because I was stumped for an answer to the medical examiner's question, "Why do you smoke?" I had absolutely no logical defense for my action.

—Before New Year's, 1968, two friends and I each put twenty dollars in an envelope. We agreed if one smoked at any time he would immediately forfeit his twenty dollars. If we all returned to smoking, sixty dollars would be donated to the Canadian Cancer Society, and if we didn't smoke for one year, our money was to be refunded.

Although two of us had smoked for thirty years and one for twenty years, none of us have returned to the habit.

—I started carrying wooden matches (I cut off the heads) and toothpicks in my pocket. Each time I craved a smoke I put one in my mouth (right in—not just sticking out) and found that the saliva formed from desiring a smoke was absorbed by chewing and sucking this wood. I didn't need that cigarette after all! The wooden match didn't taste bad, it had no calories and was not expensive, and I just repeated this cycle every time that saliva came into my mouth. After a few weeks I stopped the match chewing, but every so often when that cigarette craving returned it was back to matches.

—I told no one of my intention and had a complete carton of smokes on hand when I set out to escape them. Also I prayed for help. I'm not religious but had experienced the power of prayer in other things.

The first day I eliminated my after-breakfast cigarette, the one I enjoyed the most. The next day I did not have the one after lunch; the third day the after-dinner one was abandoned. Determined not to replace one habit with another, I deliberately avoided gum, candy, etc. Also, from the first I drank my coffee without smoking, waiting at least until it was finished before lighting up. If I went to answer the phone I left my cigarettes elsewhere. From this point on I began to eliminate each day, in order of importance, one more cigarette—in effect weaning myself.

Generally speaking, it was more bearable than I had expected. The night I cut off the last cigarette was the worst, bringing some wakeful hours. But after a week or so the acute desire to smoke left. It is now seven years since my last cigarette and it feels good.

—I decided that I had to fight a compulsion: the ritual of selecting the cleanly slim tube, tapping it on the cigarette package, using the shiny lighter and lighting up.

I believe that habits are like bundles of long twigs bound tightly together. Every time you perform the ritual of smoking you add another twig to the bundle until finally it becomes as strong as the trunk of a tree—impossible to break.

To quit I had to take twigs away, one at a time. The twigs are hours—hours away from smoking. And I lived from hour to hour, thinking of twigs.

And I reinforced my twig removal by making up a list of all things that bugged me about smoking.

—The habit had so overcome me that I couldn't answer the telephone without first lighting a cigarette. Often I had two going in different parts of the house. Then one day I set the next Monday as "Stop Smoking Day." First I went into the garden and picked two small stones very carefully, a light one and a dark-colored one. Believing that a lot of smoking pleasure lies in purely oral satisfaction, I chose the stones for their pleasant, rounded, slightly irregular surfaces and then, when I thought I couldn't bear it without a cigarette, I would suck one of the stones. (I fancied the white one as vanilla and the dark one as chocolate.) In this way I occupied my tongue during the withdrawal procedure and never had to resort to candies. Inside a couple of weeks I could go without a cigarette; inside of six months I could say I had stopped smoking permanently.

—One day, while reading an article on poverty in India, I was shocked by so much suffering, particularly among innocent little children. I tried to picture my own children in this tragic plight, and I thought how wonderful it would be under these circumstances if someone would give me enough money each month so that they would no longer have to go to bed at night hungry. Here staring at me from the magazine was a reason to stop smoking.

It was a bit rough for a few days, but the thought of saving money to help those little children eat regularly alleviated my desire to smoke. After two months I turned over my savings to a charity, and I still make regular donations.

—*First,* I told all my friends, relatives, and anybody who would listen that I was going to quit smoking. I committed myself and really did it up. I thought, the more people who know about it, the more difficult it will be to backslide.

I announced it with a big splash one New Year's Eve. I told my wife, my children, my boss, my buddies at work, I told the people I dealt with. . . . I was committed but good. I watched their smug faces telling me it wouldn't last . . . I'd soon be at it again. They bribed me, teased me, offered me cigarettes, and *every time I said "No thank you," I won a little victory for myself.*

It was these victories, one by one, that helped me win the ultimate battle. It was worth the look of bewilderment on my friends' faces when I refused their smokes. They didn't know that *because I had to say "no" to them every day* I was able to convince myself.

—For me, after twenty-eight years in the army (during the entire time I smoked), self-discipline came easily. On countless occasions when I was terrified for my life, I said to myself, "You must show no fear." This always worked.

I attended the annual "Paardeberg Day" Ball of the Royal Canadian Regiment. The festivities had begun with a noon-hour whiskey-and-soda welcome (at which I purchased two packages of cigarettes), followed by an afternoon reception at four, cocktails at seven, dinner at eight, and the ball at ten o'clock. By the cocktail hour I had emptied my silver cigarette case. I refilled it before entering the dining room. By the time the orchestra played "God Save the Queen" at one in the morning, eighteen more of the little white cylinders had gone up in smoke.

In my hotel-bound taxi I suddenly decided that forty cigarettes between lunch and bedtime was sheer madness. I knew I could never cut down, because I have a compulsive nature. I gave myself an order: "Tonight you stop smoking."

Back in the hotel, my wife suggested we have a cigarette each before turning out the lights. I showed her my case, one cigarette remaining. She suggested we break it in two or puff it turn-and-turn-about. "Take it," I said. "I have stopped smoking." I was forty-four years of age when I stopped. No candy, no drugs—nothing in the way of treatment or literature was necessary. Only two things were required: the genuine desire or will to quit—and self-discipline.

—It seemed silly at first, but the only requirement was concentration. Concentration not to inhale.

I began my experiment in January 1960, and during the days that followed I actually smoked more. My family urged me to forget the whole idea. Tempted though I was, I felt that the effort to concentrate was going to work. Because of the uncertainty I hesitated to stop completely, but kept on concentrating on not inhaling.

Shortly all my earlier doubts were dispersed. As February came to a close, so did my dependency on smoking. I was safely weaned.

—I had smoked twenty to thirty cigarettes daily for over ten years, and had a bad throat and cough.

In 1963, when living in Edmonton, my family and I drove to British Columbia to the fruit belt in the Okanagan Valley. On starting this one-week trip I decided to quit smoking. I ate substantial quantities of fruit (peaches, pears, and plums) for that week and had little craving for tobacco. Daily consumption may have been eight peaches, five pears, and twenty plums. We brought back seventeen boxes of fruit and I ate substantial quantities for the next week or so as well. The only side effect was a gastrointestinal upset, but the smoking habit was licked. I have not smoked since except for two occasions of about a month each. Tobacco smoke is very unpleasant to me now.

—The cure was simple. I asked the druggist for a bitter tonic and took a dessert spoonful in a third of a glass of water with every meal. I took it between the first course and dessert because it tasted so strong. I started this the day before I decided to quit, smoking my usual amount during that day. When I got up the next morning I kept my decision without difficulty and have never smoked since—though I did use the whole bottle of tonic.

—My eye fell on Norman Vincent Peale's book, *The Power of Positive Thinking*. I opened it at random and read his account of two New York tycoons who dropped into an empty Manhattan church at lunchtime to seek some relief from mounting tensions. I had my answer. *Church was surely one place where people did not smoke.* Moreover, these two men went to obtain relief from tension—which was my drive to smoke.

I was on the starting line to a method of quitting my

addiction. I would do it one day at a time. *I would run from one haven of safety to another*—empty churches, courtrooms, public libraries, anyplace where smoking was prohibited, anyplace where it would be easier to hold the line and divert my mind from the craving that by lunchtime was coming and going in waves of sheer torture. Even in the church I visited I came close to sneaking behind the baptismal font for a couple of drags.

Right after my lunch I took a couple of tranquilizer pills and fell asleep. Later I thought, "Good grief, this is the first time in over thirty years I haven't had a smoke before lunch." It gave me a glimmer of strength and hope to get through this ordeal. ONE DAY AT A TIME was only a few hours away. Maybe I could extend those prelunch hours to twenty-four, if I could just get through the period between lunchtime and supper.

There was a movie showing that I wanted to see and I went to keep my mind occupied. By now I was going on the basis of ONE HOUR AT A TIME. I found a seat and started to fiddle with a package of cigarettes when a notice was flashed on the screen, "Sorry, due to fire regulations, NO SMOKING ALLOWED." I got the strongest feeling that, with all this guidance I was getting, I would die on the spot if I even so much as sneaked a puff.

That night I fell asleep with the firm conviction that never again would I risk getting hooked and having to go through the agony of another day's withdrawal. I did not fear the following day, because I knew what to do—simply repeat the exact timetable. I kept this program going for about three weeks while my cravings diminished and finally disappeared entirely.

—Here is how I quit after twenty-three years—more than two packs a day on weekdays and a pack a day on weekends:

First: I set a date. There is no point in dramatically

throwing down a cigarette and saying, "I have just quit." That doesn't work.

Second: As the date approached, I said nothing about it, told no one what date it was or that a date had been set, and didn't change my smoking habits.

Third: When the time came, I avoided lingering over meals, cocktail parties, or other such gatherings, and slept as much as possible. You can't smoke when you're sleeping. The first 48 hours were the toughest—almost unbearable.

Fourth: For the first few days I used a nicotine substitute. I didn't try to see how far I could go without a cigarette but how far I could go without the substitute. When I absolutely had to have a cigarette, I took the other.

Fifth: And this is most important. After I had succeeded for a week or more, I never said, "I haven't had a cigarette in X weeks or in Y days." I just said, "I don't smoke."

Make no mistake about it, it is a damn difficult thing to do for a heavy smoker who has smoked since his teen-age days. But it can be done, and this former smoker hasn't had a cigarette, cigar, pipe, or drag from any of them for almost two years, and no longer cares to.

—I never quit smoking. I just didn't smoke for one day at a time.

I kept busy when I thought I might want a cigarette. I drank a lot of water. Sometimes I put a little lemon juice in it. I brushed my teeth more often than usual.

Did I suffer? No, because it was only for one day. Even I could do it for one day.

At the end of the day I felt fine. I thought, "I will not smoke tomorrow and maybe the agonies will start on the second day."

I followed the same routine on the second day. I found that *a cigarette does not need to accompany a cup of tea or coffee.* Furthermore, coffee can be enjoyed even more without a cigarette. The end of the second day came and still no suffering, but I was tired from keeping busy.

The third was a repeat of the other two except I didn't have to work as hard at not thinking about smoking. I even stayed up later that night.

The fourth morning came. I decided that since it was nearly the end of the week I might as well finish it.

Somehow, I have never wanted to smoke again. That was twelve years ago.

—In September 1968 my teen-age daughter, who had seen films against smoking at school, suggested I try a brand with a new-type filter. To please her I bought them. Though I didn't particularly enjoy the change, I stuck to it. I had the idea that if the body developed a craving for nicotine it could be partially satisfied and lessened gradually by using this type of cigarette. When I first started I smoked more but gradually tapered down to my former level.

One evening about four weeks later I asked my son to let me have a good cigarette for a change. He left two and I smoked them both. After so many weeks on the filter brand, I found the high tar-nicotine content of my old favorites was burning the inside of my mouth.

That was the end. I wasn't enjoying the taste of the filtered smoke and now I couldn't enjoy the unfiltered. It seemed a silly waste of time to continue.

—And a bonus—a personal story contributed by Miss Louise Fisher, who was reminded of her own experience when she typed this manuscript:

In the fall of 1966 I had a bout with flu, and cigarettes tasted so perfectly awful I stopped smoking for the duration, about four weeks. Whereupon I said to myself, "You darn fool! You haven't smoked for four weeks, why bother to start again?"

And that, literally, was how I stopped. And I've never missed it. Actually, it has heightened my appreciation of food. I always did enjoy eating, but now I can taste all the subtle flavors of fine food.

When I stopped, cigarettes were $4.40 a carton in the

supermarket and I had been smoking at least a carton a week. I decided to put away $5.00 a week which I normally would have burned, and at the end of a year I had $250 saved up. Just then, a broker friend of mine put me onto a new stock issue in December 1967. With just $150 of my nest egg I bought twenty shares (all my friend could allot me since this was a very "hot" issue) at $7.50 a share. In a little over six months the stock went up to $120 a share. I sold out for about $2,000! Money to burn? Oh no! I sold the flyer and put the proceeds into a fine blue-chip stock.

DAY FOURTEEN | *Action*

Fifty Ways to Cut Down/ Cut Out Cigarettes

It was my last cigar, it was my last cigar;
I breath'd a sigh to think, in sooth,
It was my last cigar.

Anon., *My Last Cigar* (c. 1860) A
popular college song for many years

This chapter consists of fifty pointers (actually, more than fifty separate Actions, since some pointers offer multiple Actions) to cut down on or eliminate cigarettes. Because all smokers do not smoke for the same reasons, not all tips are useful for all smokers, and some tips even contradict others. Everyone who has followed our plan up to this point knows what sort of smoker he is and what is likely to work best for him. He can choose those points that suit him.

Many of the points reiterate material found in other chapters. This has been done purposely, because this list is meant to give you in one convenient place all of the tactics and gimmicks known to us. Doubtless there are others; and certainly others will be invented. People who want to give up cigarettes have proved themselves extremely resourceful. We have deliberately omitted tricks that are too special, such as the cigarette case used by Soviet party chief Leonid I. Brezhnev. It has a timing device that allows it to be opened only every forty-five minutes. But, Brezhnev has revealed, he carries a reserve pack in his pocket just in case.

1. Before trying to quit smoking, wrap your cigarettes for at least one week as described in Day Four. Every time you want a cigarette you must unwrap the package and write down the time, what you are doing, how you feel, and how important this cigarette is to you. Almost everyone who tries this cuts down considerably on his smoking because he becomes so aware of the act.

2. A great many people unconsciously taper themselves off cigarettes before finally quitting. You can do this consciously. In addition to the wrap sheet, try the following Actions:

—Take fewer puffs of each cigarette.

—Don't smoke cigarettes all the way down—stop halfway. This eliminates a good deal of the tar, which is trapped within the first half of the cigarette, acting as a filter.

—Switch to low tar and nicotine cigarettes.

—Whatever you smoke, smoke less of it.

—Most important—DO NOT INHALE. It's the inhalation that does most of the damage.

3. If cigarettes give you a lift, try substituting chewing gum, modest exercise such as a brisk walk, or a new hobby. Stay away from very high calorie foods; drink fruit juices or low-calorie soft drinks.

4. If cigarettes relax you, try low-calorie snacks, new beverages, or undemanding social activities.

5. If you need cigarettes and crave them, the only way to get off is to stop suddenly and completely. To help yourself, try smoking a great deal more than usual for two or three days before quitting. This will make them distasteful and easier to give up. Also try switching to a brand you

don't like, one that's too strong. Let a pack get stale, then force yourself to smoke it. A good time to make the break is when you have a bad cold, when you don't really want or enjoy smoking. Then go on from there.

6. On one side of a three-by-five-inch card write down what you like about smoking and on the other side what you dislike. Look it over daily and add to it, particularly side number two.

7. What are the things you would like to buy or do, for which you don't have the money? Write them down with the costs, and divide each by what you spend on cigarettes per day. See how many days it will take you to buy what you want. That number of days without cigarettes can be your immediate goal. When you save the money you can decide if you care to start smoking again.

8. How much do you spend on cigarettes per day? Try taping that amount to a calendar each day that you don't smoke as a reminder of what you're saving.

9. Make a bet with a friend who wants to quit smoking— of a good meal, a dollar a day, or a fixed sum of money. The first one who smokes loses and pays. If you both stay off cigarettes for sixty days you can cancel the bet, or spend the money together.

10. Make a pledge to a charity—and "earn" the money from the cigarettes you don't smoke.

11. When you crave a cigarette, force yourself to wait at least three minutes before lighting up. During that time, deliberately change what you're doing; try to think about something else.

12. Make friends with an ex-smoker or with someone like yourself who wants to quit, someone you can call up when you must have a smoke.

13. Plan a date for stopping. For stress smokers a vacation is an excellent time. For some it's easiest to make a New Year's resolution. A child's birthday is a good time to

give a present of a smoke-free house. You may decide you want to give your spouse a healthier helpmeet on your wedding anniversary. But don't pick a date so far in the future that you may forget your resolve.

14. Pick a time to quit when you think you will be able to stand the tension. Make it easiest on yourself. For example, a stress-smoking woman in the throes of divorce decided not to stop until she'd readjusted to her new life. Then she could manage more easily without smoking.

15. When you've picked a "Q Day" (quit day), you may want to try tapering down in advance the number of cigarettes you smoke, so that when Q-day arrives you won't have to face a large or sudden withdrawal.

16. Never stock up on cigarettes; never buy a carton. Wait until each pack is finished before you buy the next.

17. Never carry cigarettes with you at home or work. Keep them as far away from you as possible—and hard to get at. Leave them with someone, or lock them up in a file cabinet. One man gave his cigarettes to his secretary, and was so ashamed to ask her for one that he stopped smoking at work. The rest was easy.

18. Make yourself a smoking corner and confine your smoking to that spot. Be sure that it is far from anyone interesting and preferably in an uncomfortable setting. No TV, radio, record player, or telephone. No books, magazines, or newspapers.

19. If you are a solitary smoker, force yourself to smoke only with others. If you are a social smoker, smoke only when alone.

20. Never carry matches or a lighter.

21. Put all your ashtrays in closets, or fill them with objects like nuts in the shell or fruit. Instead of smoking you can eat something—but first you must remove the shell or skin, which gives you something to do with your hands.

22. Change your brand of cigarettes every other day—and try to go to a lower tar and nicotine brand each time.

23. Never say "I quit smoking," because then if you smoke you'll feel defeated. It's better to try to think of yourself as, and to call yourself, a nonsmoker. Even if, like Dr. Hayakawa, you've smoked for thirty years, you can say "I don't smoke."

24. Always ask yourself, "Do I really want this cigarette, or is this just a reflex?"

25. Each day try putting off lighting your first cigarette by thirty minutes.

26. Decide that you will smoke only on even- or odd-numbered hours.

27. Eventually you may work up to smoking only on odd- or even-numbered days.

28. Try going to bed early and rising a half-hour earlier than usual to avoid hurrying through breakfast and rushing to work.

29. Keep your hands occupied. Try playing a musical instrument (a recorder or harmonica is cheap and easy), knitting, whittling, working jigsaw puzzles, or fingering worry beads.

30. Get a couple of smooth stones or small marbles, wash them, and suck on one when you want a smoke.

31. Try chewing on a flavored toothpick instead of smoking. Remove the heads from some wooden kitchen matches. Put several headless matches in your mouth and chew on them.

32. Keep a flask of spicy soup or tomato juice cocktail handy for when you get that craving feeling in the chest.

33. Try your own aversive therapy. Twice a day, smoke one cigarette after another as fast as you can without interruption, until you can't bear another drag. Then after a few

days cut this down to once a day, and don't smoke between these episodes.

34. When you want to smoke, take a shower. You can't smoke in the shower.

35. Or try taking a bath. One woman made the break successfully by passing most of one weekend in the tub.

36. Spend time in places where smoking is forbidden: churches, public libraries, courtrooms, public conveyances, theaters. These places are becoming more numerous and now include many restaurants, hotels, and shops, as laws to protect nonsmokers are being passed in many cities and states.

37. Start expanding your lungs through increased athletic activity, depending on your age and physical condition and always with your doctor's permission. Walk a half-hour a day. Especially try walking immediately after a meal, as a substitute for the desired smoke.

38. Some people gain a few pounds after they quit. This is usually temporary. But, if you do gain, don't try to take off weight until you feel comfortable dieting. Remember, though, once you lick the cigarette habit, it's much easier to control other habits, including overeating.

39. If you feel you need professional help or support, see your doctor. He may prescribe a mild tranquilizer to assist you through the first few days. Certainly see him if you have any persistent symptoms that might be related to smoking or quitting.

40. When you stop smoking, visit your dentist and have him clean your teeth. The investment may make you reluctant to start smoking again.

41. When you decide to quit, announce it widely among your friends and family. This kind of social commitment helps many stick to their resolution.

42. If you feel irritable or tense, shut your eyes and count

backward from ten to zero while imagining yourself descending a flight of stairs or watching the sun slowly sink beyond the western horizon.

43. Figure the cost of cigarettes for two months. Purchase a money order for this amount and give it to your spouse or a close friend to hold for sixty days. If during that time you smoke—they get to keep the money. If not, you get it back.

44. Shake yourself out of your old routines. Seek new activities, or perform old activities in new ways. Break up fixed habit patterns; go to work a different way. Socialize with new people who don't smoke. Take a trip.

45. If you're a kitchen smoker in the morning, volunteer your services to a school, hospital, or volunteer organization. Get yourself out of the house.

46. Stock up on light reading materials, crossword puzzles, and vacation brochures for places you'll be able to afford on the money you'll save by not smoking, and read these during coffee breaks.

47. For some people it's easiest not to smoke in bed; they sleep more, to help themselves quit. But for others occupation is the answer to temptation; they must keep active and busy.

48. Don't quit permanently. Just quit for today—and tomorrow—and the next day, until you've established your new habit.

49. If you wear pants, try taping your cigarettes to your thigh. You can smoke whenever you want to, but you'll have to take your pants off first.

50. At home put your cigarettes in the most inconvenient places, and far from matches or lighter. One man kept his in the mailbox and forced himself to smoke only outside his house.

DAYS FIFTEEN THROUGH SEVENTY

Ods me, I marvel what pleasure or felicity
they have in taking their roguish tobacco.
It is good for nothing but to choke a man,
and fill him full of smoke and embers.

> Ben Jonson
> *Every Man in His Humour*

DAYS FIFTEEN THROUGH SEVENTY

Follow-Up Activity

Now you may have been off cigarettes for 48 hours. You're really over the worst part, you know. And if you fall off the wagon, go back and reread Day Eleven, Section 2: "Quitting Is a Process." Above all, don't feel guilty. Remember, there are always mistakes in learning. There will always be errors in relearning. That, as the professor said, is why they plot learning as a curve not a straight line.

To help you continue your new habit of not smoking, fill out the scorecard reproduced at the back of this book. Anyone who continues for thirty days has probably relearned his habit. After sixty days there is no real desire to smoke.

Yet, when Dr. Fredrickson surveyed some of his former group members who had successfully become nonsmokers, he found that some had started to smoke again. Why? Not out of need or even desire—but out of curiosity. A typical comment: "I tried a cigarette to see why I had wanted to smoke in the first place. I didn't like it. In fact, it made me dizzy. So I tried another—and another." Dr. Fredrickson thinks that a few people (they're extremely rare) who were once smokers can, after they've stopped, take a cigarette or two now and then without becoming hooked. But for almost all smokers the best advice is never to try this. "It's something like a reformed alcoholic taking a drink," Dr. Fredrickson says. "It amost inevitably leads to another." In other words, don't trifle with success.

But always remember that backsliding is normal in re-learning. Once you've managed to stay off cigarettes for even two Days, you can manage to do it again and for a longer time on the next try. Quitting *is* a process, and you're well on the way to the fresh air at the end of the tunnel. Now. do you want to try for three Days?

YOUR NONSMOKING SCORECARD

Neither do thou lust after that
tawney tobacco.

> Ben Jonson
> *Bartholomew Fair*

To aid you in your resolve and to act as a daily reminder,
we include an eight-week calendar on which to check off
your nonsmoking days and to keep track of the money you
save. After eight weeks you'll be so far out of the woods
that you never need wander back.

The scorecards begin at Day Three, your first nonsmoking
Day after the critical first 48 hours. At the end of 58 Days
a pack-a-day smoker will have saved about thirty dollars.
Take the money and treat yourself with it. Buy anything
except tobacco in any form. Don't give up.

If, in a moment of weakness, you break down and have a
cigarette, don't be discouraged. Just start over. Every cigarette you don't smoke, every day you don't smoke, is that
much less smoke in your lungs. It helps put you one up
statistically.

Remember: If at first you don't succeed, quit, quit again.

1. Check off each day you don't smoke. It adds up.
2. Mark down how much you save each day by not smoking. That adds up too.
3. Keep the scorecard with you, or cut on the dotted line and carry the weekly ticket in your pocket or pocketbook or wallet instead of cigarettes.
4. If you're tempted, pull it out and look at your progress—do you want to spoil that record?
5. Think of swimming across a pool without gasping, or running up stairs without wheezing.
6. Ten million people have quit smoking in the last five years. So can you.
7. At the very least, you stop damaging yourself.
8. At best, if you quit and stay quit, it can be as if you never smoked.
9. You increase your chances of not dying younger than you should.
10. Probably, you'll get fewer colds and sore throats.
11. You'll find your breathing's improved. You won't run out of breath so fast after doing something physical.

Figure 1

DAY 3	DAY 4	DAY 5
Saved $	Saved $	Saved $ . . . . .
DAY 6	**DAY 7** Who says I can't quit ?	**DAY 8**
Saved $	Saved $	Saved $ . . . . .

DAY 9

Saved $ . . . . .

Total saved:

$ . . . . . .

Congratulations!
You have Not Smoked for 9 Days.
See? You can do it!

Figure 2

DAY 10 Yes, I will not smoke today. Saved $	**DAY 11** Saved $	**DAY 12** Saved $ . . . . .
DAY 13 Saved $	**DAY 14** Saved $	**DAY 15** Saved $ . . . . .
DAY 16 Saved $ . . . . . Total saved: $	Sixteen whole Days! You've proved it can be done. The trick now is not to let down. Remember, it took more than this to get the habit in the first place.	

Figure 3

DAY 17 Saved $	**DAY** 18 Saved $	**DAY** 19 Saved $ . . . . .
DAY 20 Saved $	**DAY** 21 Saved $	**DAY** 22 Saved $ . . . . .
DAY 23 Saved $ . . . . . Total saved: $	Twenty-three Days of Not Smoking! If you are proud of yourself, you've got a right to be. Don't blow it now.	

Figure 4

DAY 24	DAY 25	DAY 26
	I feel better already.	
Saved $	Saved $	Saved $ . . . . .
DAY 27	**DAY 28**	**DAY 29**
Saved $	Saved $	Saved $ . . . . .

DAY 30	Thirty Days of Not Smoking! It tells you something about yourself: you're stronger than the habit; you don't need it. Now stick to your guns!
Saved $.	
Total saved: $	

Figure 5

DAY 31	DAY 32	DAY 33
Saved $	Saved $	Saved $ . . . . .

DAY 34	DAY 35	DAY 36
	I should pollute my own lungs?	
Saved $	Saved $	Saved $ . . . . .

DAY 37

Saved $ . . . . .

Total saved:

$ . . . . .

You have now lived more than
five whole weeks without a
cigarette.
You're over the worst part.
But don't take it for granted;
it's still easy to slide back
on a bad day.
So keep your guard up.

Figure 6

DAY 38 I am not a dummy. Saved $	**DAY 39** Saved $	**DAY 40** Saved $ . . . . .
DAY 41 Saved $	**DAY 42** Saved $	**DAY 43** I am not a patsy. Saved $ . . . . .
DAY 44 Saved $ . . . . . Total saved: $	Over six weeks of Not Smoking! Do you realize that cigarette manufacturers are spending hundreds of millions of dollars coaxing, cajoling, encouraging you to smoke? You are singlehandedly fighting off a multimillion-dollar attack. Keep it up.	

Figure 7

DAY 45 I am not a weakling. Saved $	**DAY 46** Saved $	**DAY 47** Saved $ . . . . .
DAY 48 Saved $	**DAY 49** Saved $	**DAY 50** I am not a smoker. Saved $ . . . . .
DAY 51 Saved $ . . . . . Total saved: $	Fifty-one Days of Not Smoking—nearly two months. Now you know you're a nonsmoker.	

Figure 8

DAY 52 Saved $	**DAY 53** Saved $	**DAY 54** Saved $ . . . . .
DAY 55 Saved $	**DAY 56** My declaration of independence: Saved $	**DAY 57** I can live without it. Saved $ . . . . .

DAY 58

Saved $ . . . . .

Total saved:

$ . . . . .

That's nearly two months
of Not Smoking.
You've proved you can
live without it.
Now live.
Without it.

More nice things to look forward to:
   —No more nicotine hangover in the morning.
   —No more coughing up phlegm the way you used to.
   —You won't have to feel guilty about smoking in front
of the kids anymore.
   —You'll run and swim and ski and walk faster and far-
ther. You'll no longer be an addict.

Now you know you can live without smoking.
   It wasn't easy, but you've done it.
   There's no reason for you ever to have another cigarette.
   After all, no one can make you smoke. Don't let your
guard down; don't unthinkingly have a cigarette; don't slide
back by accident; don't let a bad day give you an excuse to
smoke.
   (But if you do, don't forget: If at first you don't succeed,
quit, quit again.)
   And if you want another of these scorecards, it's yours
free. Just send a card to: Scorecard, Rockville, Md., 20852.

*This scorecard was created by the National Clearinghouse for
Smoking and Health. It is reproduced with permission.*

FOR THE FUTURE

Thus they sit talking, and taking Tobacco some
two hours, and until their pipes be all spent (for
by them they measure the time of this their solemn
conference) no man must interrupt . . . for this is
their religion. . . .

> Lawrence Keymis (1596)
> 16th-century English Explorer

Most people who have been habitual smokers will, once
they've quit cigarettes for two months, never smoke again.

But if a former smoker does begin smoking because of
unusual stress or some other reason, there's no need to
panic. If this should happen to you, remember the lessons
you've learned from this book, go back and look up the tips
and other helps, and start to quit again. It will be easier and
much less frightening the second time.

APPENDICES

Herein is not only a great vanity but a
great contempt of God's good gifts, that
the sweetness of man's breath, being a
good gift of God, should be wilfully
corrupted by this stinking smoke.

>   James I of England
>   *A Counterblaste to Tobacco*

Following are the highlights of the latest research into the
health hazards of smoking and the benefits of quitting. Even
if you think yourself knowledgeable in this subject, you will
probably find a great deal of new and conclusive information in these pages that you have never seen anywhere else.

APPENDIX A:

Smokers Die Younger of All Causes

For thy sake, Tobacco, I
Would do anything but die.

> Charles Lamb
> *A Farewell to Tobacco*

The most visible and conclusive manifestation of the health effects of smoking is in the comparative death rates of smokers and nonsmokers.

Smokers as a group die younger and suffer more deaths at every age level—from all causes—than do people who have never smoked. The death rate (number of deaths per hundred thousand) of smokers from all causes increases with the number of cigarettes smoked per day, the number of years the smoker has been smoking, and the earlier the age at which he started.

In seven major prospective studies * of almost two million people, cigarette-smoking men had a death rate about

* A prospective study is one that follows the health histories of a designated group of people during a projected period of time, usually several years, into the future.

70 percent above that of nonsmokers. Several studies also show a parallel but lesser relationship between cigarette smoking and increased death rates of women. The death rate for a given number of cigarettes smoked is higher among people who say they inhale than it is among those who say they don't.

For groups of men smoking fewer than ten cigarettes per day, the death rate is about 35 percent higher than for non-smokers; between ten and nineteen cigarettes per day it is 70 percent higher; between twenty and thirty cigarettes per day the death rate is 95 percent higher, and for those who smoke more than forty cigarettes a day the death rate is 125 percent higher than for nonsmokers. For men who started smoking before the age of twenty, the death rate is substantially higher than for those who started after age twenty-five.

From a prospective study of more than one million American men and women over age thirty, 36,975 matched pairs of male smokers and nonsmokers were selected by computer. They were matched by race, height, nativity, residence, occupation, education, marital status, consumption of alcohol, and eleven other criteria.

After three years, among these pairs of men:

—Twice as many smokers had died as nonsmokers, 1,385 as against 662.

—654 smokers had died of coronary heart disease, compared with 304 nonsmokers.

—There were 110 lung cancer deaths among smokers, contrasted with only 12 among nonsmokers.

Life Expectancy: Male

A man of twenty-five who smokes two packs a day can expect to live (on the average) 40.3 years, or until just past age sixty-five. But a nonsmoker aged twenty-five can expect to live 48.6 years, more than eight years longer, until he is seventy-three-plus.

At age fifty the two-pack-a-day smoker has an average expectancy of only 19.3 years of life, until age sixty-nine. But nonsmokers can expect to live 25.6 years, until past seventy-five.

Death Rates: Female

Women who smoke cigarettes have a significantly higher death rate than those who have never smoked regularly. As with men, the relationship between death and smoking is directly related to the number of cigarettes smoked and the length of time smoked. The ratios are somewhat lower. One reason is that many women have become habitual cigarette smokers more recently than men. The mortality figures show that women are only slightly less vulnerable than men to the health hazards of cigarettes.

Excess Deaths

There is a normal death rate at every age. It follows, therefore, that there is a normal number of deaths at every age. Deaths above the expected number are called "excess" or unnecessary deaths. For men between the ages of thirty-five and fifty-nine who smoke cigarettes, the excess deaths account for one out of every three deaths. In other words, if no one smoked there would be one-third fewer male deaths between ages thirty-five and fifty-nine, the most productive years.

Several years ago an expert calculated the number of excess deaths associated with smoking cigarettes and compared them with the total of all deaths in this country caused by infections, motor vehicles, suicide, homicide, and diabetes. The two figures are almost identical, as follows:

AMERICAN BALANCE OF HAZARDS TO LIFE (1966)

EXCESS DEATHS FROM TOBACCO SMOKING

Lung cancer 41,012
Other cancers (of larynx, bladder) 28,045
Coronary disease 145,956
Other vascular disease 42,821
All other causes (emphysema, bronchitis, etc.) .. 43,726

Total Excess Deaths from Tobacco Smoking .. 301,560

DEATHS FROM SELECTED CAUSES

All infections 128,180
Tuberculosis .... (7,590)*
Pneumonia and influenza .... (64,230)
All accidents 112,300
Motor vehicles .... (53,280)
Diabetes 35,380
Suicide 20,160
Homicide 11,210

Balancing Total 307,230

* Figures in parentheses are included in previous categories. (Compiled by R. T. Ravenholt, M.D., of Agency for International Development, Washington, D.C.)

Disability

Cigarette smokers in the United States have higher rates of disability than do nonsmokers. As in mortality, there is a normal or expected rate of disability. A national health survey by the U.S. Public Health Service calculated that in a single year cigarette smoking caused an *excess* of:

-—77 million man-days lost from work.
—88 million man-days spent ill in bed.
—306 million man-days of restricted activity.

For men between ages forty-five and sixty-four, more than 25 percent of the number of days of disability are associated with cigarette smoking.

Another study showed that women who smoke cigarettes, housewives and those with paid jobs, spend 17 percent more days ill in bed than women who have never smoked.

Chronic Illness

Taking the chronic disease rate of people who had never smoked cigarettes as the baseline, the National Clearinghouse for Smoking and Health estimated that "there are eleven million more chronic cases of illness yearly in this country than there would be" (if no one smoked).

The same study calculated that "there are 280,000 more persons who report a heart condition," plus one million more cases of chronic bronchitis and/or emphysema, 1.8 million more cases of sinusitis, and one million more cases of peptic ulcer than there would be if no one ever smoked cigarettes.

Benefits of Stopping

In the seven prospective studies, ex-smokers who had stopped smoking before being enrolled in studies had a death rate 40 percent higher than those who had never smoked, but those who were still smoking had a death rate 70 percent higher than that of nonsmokers.

Of course, many people stop smoking only when they have active symptoms of disease. Excluding those who have already contracted an irreversible disease, the death rate of those who stop smoking begins to decline immediately and, after ten years, the former pack-a-day smokers' death rate is almost the same as if they had never smoked.

APPENDIX B:

Heart Attacks, Circulatory Diseases, and Strokes

Tobacco is the delight of Dutchmen,
as it diffuses a torpor and pleasing
stupefaction.

> Edmund Burke
> *The Sublime and the Beautiful*

Although most smokers were first made aware of the health hazards of cigarettes in relation to lung cancer, a far greater number of cigarette-smoking deaths are caused by heart attacks, circulatory diseases, and strokes.

On the average, all smokers have a 70 percent greater risk of developing coronary heart disease than have non-smokers. But as in other smoking-related diseases and deaths, the amount of damage is directly proportional to the number of cigarettes smoked, the earlier the age at which the smoker started, and the number of years he has continued. Men aged forty to forty-nine, smoking more than two packs a day, have the highest heart attack risk—more than five times (500 percent) the risk of nonsmokers.

It is also true that giving up smoking sharply diminishes the risk of heart attacks, strokes, and other circulatory diseases. This begins to happen within one year after stopping. Dr. Fredrickson believes that the "benefits appear to be immediate and substantial, particularly for the middle-aged heavy cigarette smoking male with clinical coronary disease because of his very high risk of sudden death resulting in part from the trigger effect of the cigarette habit."

A study of British doctors aged thirty-five to sixty-four has been going on since 1951. During this time many of the doctors have given up cigarette smoking. But British men have in general continued to smoke cigarettes. (About one-third of British doctors now smoke cigarettes, compared with two-thirds of all men in the general population.) During this period, deaths from coronary heart disease *dropped* by 6 percent among the British doctors, but *rose* by 32 percent in British men of the same ages. An estimated eighty British doctors who would have died of a smoking-related disease each year did not die, simply because they stopped smoking cigarettes. In the same groups there was a similar effect on the lung cancer death rate (see Appendix C).

Risk Factors

Several major risk factors have been identified in heart attacks. Three leading risk factors are 1) a high level of cholesterol in the blood; 2) high blood pressure; and 3) physical inactivity/obesity. Smoking cigarettes is a fourth risk factor as important as any of these.

Each of these risk factors increases chances of a heart attack. People who smoke only cigarettes but have none of the other three factors have a death rate from heart attack 70 percent greater than that of nonsmokers. If all four risk factors are present, the risk goes up to three times (300 percent) that of persons without any risk factors.

Artery Disease

The arteries of cigarette smokers contain a great number of fatty plaques, which adhere to the walls and clog circulation. This condition is known as atherosclerosis, a form of arteriosclerosis, and is thought to predispose the sufferer to heart attacks.

One study found that the wall of the blood vessels tended to thicken with age. But thickening was considerably greater in smokers than in nonsmokers, and was directly related to the number of cigarettes smoked.

As noted in Day Six, cigarette smoking causes the walls of the heart to contract more strongly and more often, increases the heartbeat, and thereby increases the heart's requirement for more blood-borne oxygen. If a smoker has coronary artery disease (which many may have without symptoms), the arteries simply can't carry enough blood to the heart. The oxygen deficit is multiplied because in smokers' blood, as we've seen, oxygen is replaced up to 15 percent by dangerous carbon monoxide. Dr. Fredrickson says, "This 'double-barreled' nicotine–carbon monoxide effect is probably responsible for predisposing patients with coronary artery disease to arrhythmia formation [irregular heartbeat] and triggering sudden death."

For people who already have some damage to the coronary arteries of the heart, smoking cigarettes accelerates and continues the damage "and therefore contributes to sudden death from CHD [coronary heart disease]," according to the surgeon general. The lack of oxygen in the blood may also contribute to the development of atherosclerosis.

Moreover, smoking cigarettes damages the lungs, so a smoker takes in less air with each breath than a nonsmoker. This further diminishes the amount of available oxygen called for by his overworked heart.

Another mechanism related to smoking affects the platelets, the part of the blood that causes clots. Smoking seems to cause the platelets to adhere, "which might contribute to acute thrombus [clot] formation," according to the Surgeon General of the U.S. Public Health Service.

Strokes

Some of the same mechanisms that increase the risk of heart attacks (arteriosclerosis and blood clots) also increase the danger of strokes among cigarette smokers. This is especially true for male cigarette smokers aged forty-five to fifty-four. This group had a death rate from strokes about 50 percent higher than nonsmokers of the same age. Women who smoked cigarettes in this group had a stroke death rate 100 percent higher than that of women who did not smoke.

In strokes, as in coronary heart disease, the danger of smoking cigarettes seems to be related to the amount of arteriosclerosis already present. But since smoking seems to increase arteriosclerosis, the risk continues to rise with continued smoking. Many patients who suffer strokes have arteriosclerotic heart disease as well, and a significant number die of heart attacks.

APPENDIX C:

Smoking and Cancer

. . . 'tis a plague, a mischief, a violent purger
of goods, lands, health; hellish, devilish,
and damned tobacco, the ruin and overthrow
of body and soul.

Robert Burton
Anatomy of Melancholy

Lung Cancer

When a smoker worries about his health, the focus of his
concern is apt to be lung cancer, and with good reason.
Among two-pack-a-day United States cigarette smokers,
the rate of lung cancer is from fifteen to twenty-three times
that of nonsmokers; in Great Britain it is more than thirty
times.*

And lung cancer is about 94 percent fatal.

The rate of lung cancer and of deaths from this disease,
has risen so fast in the past thirty years that doctors all over
the world consider it an epidemic. Almost all of the increase
has been in cigarette smokers.

* The British Royal College of Physicians says, "The higher British
rate may be due to the British habit of smoking cigarettes to a shorter
stub length . . . and to the greater exposure of British men to air polluted by domestic and industrial smoke."

In the United States, currently, about seventy-two thousand people die of lung cancer each year. It is the single most deadly form of cancer and by itself causes more United States deaths than all automobile accidents. Yet a few decades ago deaths from lung cancer were rare. The same is true in Great Britain. There the disease and the deaths it causes are more than twice as prevalent as in this country.

In 1971 the United States Surgeon General stated that "cigarette smoking is the main cause of lung cancer in men." Official medical and scientific opinion in nine other countries—Denmark, France, Australia, Finland, Sweden, Holland, Canada, Great Britain, and New Zealand—concurs.

But there is a comforting corollary for those who are able to stop smoking. "[Their] risk of lung cancer decreases with time almost to the level of nonsmokers; the time required is dependent on the degree of exposure," says an American Cancer Society publication.

See, for example, that study of British doctors aged thirty-five to sixty-four, between 1951 and 1965. During that period, while the lung cancer death rate for all men aged thirty-five to sixty-four in England and Wales *rose* by 7 percent, among British doctors the lung cancer death rate *dropped* by 38 percent.

Lung Cancer in Women

There is still considerable difference between lung cancer death rates of men and women. The reasons: It takes years of smoking to produce lung cancer in a human being, and heavy smoking among women is still concentrated in the younger age groups in which lung cancer is least prevalent. Too, women generally smoke less of each cigarette than men, thus avoiding the heavy concentration of nicotine and tar in the last part. Women also inhale less often and not as deeply as men, and smoke filter-tipped cigarettes with less tar and nicotine.

However, the lung cancer death rate has increased more than four times (400 percent) in American women since 1930 and is rising faster among women than among men. An English doctor calculated about ten years ago that the lifetime consumption of cigarettes among forty-seven-year-old men was four times as great as among forty-seven-year-old women, and that the male lung cancer death rate at that age was five times as great as among women. In other words, there may be a slight hormonal difference in the susceptibility of men and women to lung cancer, but not very much.

Dangerous Occupations

Some lung cancer is caused by things other than cigarettes. The risk is four times as great among uranium miners as in the general population, for instance, but it is ten times greater among uranium miners who smoke than among those who don't. In a seventeen-year study of 3,414 uranium miners there were sixty-two lung cancer deaths—but only two of these were nonsmokers.

There were twenty-four lung cancer deaths in a group of 370 asbestos workers in twenty years, about seven times the average. *All* of the deaths were in cigarette smokers. The great disproportion indicates a probable multiplication effect between inhaling asbestos and cigarette smoke. None of the eighty-seven pipe and cigar smokers in this group died of lung cancer.

There is also an increased risk of lung cancer among people who work with arsenic, chromium, nickel, coal, natural gas, and graphite. But always the risk is very much greater for those who smoke cigarettes.

Air Pollution

Does air pollution by itself cause lung cancer? Studies say probably not, or very, very little—so far. In Iceland, a country with unusually pure air, a scientist noted in 1950 the beginning of a rise in lung cancer as the people had begun to smoke more cigarettes. He predicted that a large increase in lung cancer deaths would occur in ten to twenty years if cigarette consumption continued to climb. It climbed; and there was an increase of 30 percent in male lung cancer and 52 percent in female.

City dwellers get more lung cancer than farmers—but heavy-smoking rural residents get ten to fifteen times as much lung cancer as their nonsmoking neighbors.

Filter Tips

Switching to filter tips is somewhat of a safeguard, according to two recent studies. At Roswell Park Memorial Institute in Buffalo, a study of 974 lung cancer cases concluded that smokers who switched to filter tips had a lower risk of developing lung cancer. But heavy smokers, even of filtered cigarettes, still had a lung cancer death risk five times that of nonsmokers.

In another study of 552 patients with lung cancer, matched with an equal number of controls, Dr. Ernest Wynder and associates found that those who had switched to filters ten years earlier had a lower risk of lung cancer than those continuing to smoke an equal number of nonfilter cigarettes.

Critics have said that lung cancer evidence is "only statistical." This is not true: it is also experimental, pathological, and clinical. Statistical analysis is the basis of most disease control, of course, but the evidence analyzed in cigarettes and lung cancer is very broad, involving as it does literally millions of people and animals.

There is also the criticism that too wide a variety of diseases is attributed to cigarettes. But cigarette smoke is not a single chemical. It is a mixture of several thousand chemicals, many of which are known to be harmful and thirty to be specifically cancer causing. Actually, it is unreasonable to suppose that this huge number of chemicals would produce only one kind of disease. Cigarette smoke is more like the great London fog of 1952, which greatly increased the death rate for many diseases, especially respiratory and coronary diseases.

Others have advanced the theory that there is some inherited tendency both to smoke and to get lung cancer. But of course this is easily disproved by the fact that many British doctors stopped smoking and their lung cancer death rate dropped.

There's no gainsaying the fact that, as the Surgeon General said, "Cigarette smoking is the main cause of lung cancer in men [and] a cause of lung cancer in women."

Other Cancers Caused by Smoking

Most smokers think of lung cancer as the only cancer caused by smoking. But numerous studies show that smoking tobacco—not only cigarettes—causes or is strongly associated with cancers of the larynx, mouth, esophagus, and urinary bladder as well.

Cancer of the Larynx

Cancer of the larynx strikes men most often in the fifty-five to seventy age group. Cigarette smokers' risk of dying of this disease is up to eighteen times that of nonsmokers. Pipe and cigar smokers' risk is somewhat less, seven to ten times that of nonsmokers.

Autopsy studies have revealed a clear dose relationship between the number of cigarettes smoked and cellular changes in the larynxes of men who did not die of laryngeal cancer. Every pack-or-more-a-day smoker had cells which were considered precancerous. The number of such cells was in direct proportion to the number of cigarettes smoked. Seventy-five percent of the nonsmokers had no precancerous cells at all, and those who did had very few. In the men who had quit smoking, 40 percent had abnormal cells which were in the process of disappearing and being replaced by normal cells.

N.B.: Cancer of the larynx is often cured, usually by surgery which removes the larynx, the main organ of speech. The cured patients can be taught a new method of speech but must live with a permanent opening in their throats.

Surgeon General's Conclusion. "Cigarette smoking is a significant factor in the causation of cancer of the larynx. . . . The magnitude of the risk for pipe and cigar smokers is about the same order as that for cigarette smokers, or possibly slightly lower."

Mouth Cancer

The large prospective studies show four times as many mouth cancers (cancers of the lip, tongue, floor of the mouth, hard palate, etc.) in smokers as would be expected among the population as a whole. A recent study shows an even greater increase in mouth cancer among women smokers.

Mouth cancers have a high cure rate because they are readily seen and are often treated at an early stage. Of one series of 117 patients cured of mouth cancers, 43 quit smoking but 74 continued to smoke. All remained free of symptoms for three years. Then 24 of the 74 smokers developed new cancers of the mouth, but only 4 of the 43 who had quit smoking developed cancer a second time. Thus, the repeat rate of mouth cancer was four times as great among smokers as among those who stopped smoking.

Pipe smoking has long been recognized as a cause of lip cancer. Pipe and cigar smoking both contribute to cancer at other sites in the mouth.

Surgeon General's Conclusion. "Smoking is a significant factor in the development of cancer of the oral cavity and . . . pipe smoking, alone or in conjunction with other forms of tobacco use, is causally related to cancer of the lip."

Cancer of the Esophagus

Cigarette smokers have a risk of dying of esophageal cancer about two to six times that of nonsmokers, depending on the number of cigarettes smoked—and on the amount of alcohol drunk. Alcohol increases the risk, for the known cancer-causing chemicals in cigarette smoke dissolve in alcohol, and in this form they more readily penetrate tissues. Thus, when swallowed in alcohol, they are apt to permeate the walls of the esophagus. This has been demonstrated experimentally in animals.

A study of the esophagi of 1,268 men who died of causes other than esophageal cancer showed that precancerous cells were found much more frequently in the tissues of smokers than in nonsmokers.

Surgeon General's Conclusion. "Cigarette smoking is associated with the development of cancer of the esophagus. The risk . . . among pipe and/or cigar smokers is greater than that for nonsmokers and [about the same] as for cigarette smokers, or perhaps slightly lower. [There is also] an association [with] alcohol consumption and alcohol consumption may interact with cigarette smoking. This combination of exposures is associated with especially high rates of cancer of the esophagus."

Cancer of the Urinary Bladder and Kidney

A number of experiments in animals and human beings show that the urine of smokers contains a chemical known to cause bladder cancer which is also found in cigarette smoke. Other chemicals in the urine of smokers indicate that the metabolism of tryptophan, an amino acid normally found in the body, is altered, creating some chemicals which can cause cancer.

Studies have shown a higher incidence of cancer of the urinary bladder among smokers, and a higher death rate from this disease among smokers than among nonsmokers. The relative risk, as compared with nonsmokers, of a smoker's contracting bladder cancer ranges up to more than seven times normal among all smokers, and above ten times normal in heavy smokers. In the seven prospective studies, smokers of one pack or more of cigarettes per day had a death rate from bladder cancer about three and one-half to five and one-half times that of the total population.

Smokers also have a higher risk of kidney cancer, ranging from about one and one-half to two and one-half times normal.

Surgeon General's Summary and Conclusions. "Epidemiological studies have demonstrated an association of cigarette smoking with cancer of the urinary bladder among men.

"Clinical and pathological studies have suggested that tobacco smoking may be related to alterations in the metabolism of tryptophan and may in this way contribute to the development of urinary tract cancer."

APPENDIX D:

Emphysema, Chronic Bronchitis, and Other Noncancerous Lung Diseases

Have you a coffin nail on you?

O. Henry (W. S. Porter)

"When patients with bronchitis are asked if they have a cough they not infrequently reply, 'Yes, like everyone else.' They do not realize that people with healthy lungs have no cough and produce no phlegm," as the Royal College of Physicians reports.*

Chronic bronchitis appears, with emphysema of the lung, much or most of the time in cigarette smokers. Together they are known as Chronic Obstructive Broncho-pulmonary Disease (COBD), and they have been increasing sharply.

A recent study was made of the lungs of 1,443 American men and 388 women. The technique used was first to examine the tissues and then match the results with the known

---

* SMOKING AND HEALTH NOW: *A New Report and Summary on Health from the Royal College of Physicians*, London, Pitman Medical & Scientific Publishing Co., 1971, page 69.

smoking histories of the people. Among those smoking less than a pack a day, only 13.1 percent had no emphysema and 11.7 percent had advanced disease. Among the twenty-cigarettes-a-day or more group, a tiny 0.3 percent were free of emphysema and a large 19.2 percent had advanced disease. The figures were practically reversed for the non-smokers. Ninety percent had no emphysema, and there were no advanced cases.

Chronic bronchitis is "the chronic recurrent excessive mucus secretion of the bronchial tree." Its two symptoms are 1) a chronic cough, which produces 2) sputum. The latter may be clear, but often contains pus, because people with chronic bronchitis are highly susceptible to lung infection. Bronchitis is perhaps the most common result of smoking. Teen-agers who smoke only five cigarettes a day cough and spit almost as much as an adult heavy smoker. A recent study among New Haven, Connecticut, high school students found functional changes in the lungs of those who had been smoking for only a few years. Coughing, phlegm, and shortness of breath were much more common among teen-age smokers than nonsmokers.

Pulmonary emphysema destroys the walls between tiny air sacs in the lung where oxygen is absorbed into the blood. As the walls break down, the sacs become larger—and fewer in number. The total lung surface from which oxygen can be absorbed thus shrinks, and more and more breaths are needed to keep the body oxygenated. A normal adult uses about 5 percent of his energy in breathing. A person with advanced emphysema uses up to 80 percent of his strength gasping for oxygen.

These diseases are not only disabling; they often kill. United States deaths from COBD went up from only 2,666 in 1945 to 30,390 in 1968 (nearly twelve times as many). In England, with only a quarter of our population, the death rate from COBD is four times as high (the total is above thirty thousand). In that country 35 million man-days are lost from work because of COBD—ten to twelve times the number of days forfeited in labor disputes. The majority of COBD victims are smokers. A recent study in Northern Ireland estimated that if the entire population of the country had the same death rate from chronic bronchitis as that of its nonsmokers, fewer than half of the deaths (45 percent) from COBD would have occurred.

Air Pollution

Certainly some of these deaths are caused by air pollution, but the major cause is cigarettes. The two together are probably more lethal than either one separately.

Actually, emphysema is rather rare among a population of nonsmokers who live in the areas of California with the highest air pollution. The same is true in Great Britain, where the big killer is chronic bronchitis—it's about thirty to forty times more deadly there than it is here. And, again, air pollution seems to affect primarily those with chronic bronchitis, almost all of whom are heavy smokers, according to the English medical journal *The Lancet*.

How COBD Starts

When cigarette smoke is inhaled for two to five seconds, about 80 to 90 percent stays in the body. What happens to the smoke in people is not precisely known because of the impossibility of doing research in living human beings. However, in animals the larger particles in smoke tar are deposited in the upper bronchial tree; the smaller particles lodge farther down. It seems probable that the gases in smoke stay in the upper branches.

Autopsies were made of the lungs of 1,340 people who had died of various causes and for whom complete smoking histories were available. A section of each of the four major lobes was taken and slides of the material were put in random order so that the scientists did not know whose slides they were reading.

After being checked microscopically, the results of pairs of smokers and nonsmokers were compared. Pathological changes in the lungs were greater for:

1. The older cigarette smoker than the younger cigarette smoker.

2. The one-half-pack-a-day smoker than the "never smoked."

3. The one-pack-a-day smoker than the one-half-pack-a-day smoker.

4. The two-pack-a-day smoker than the one-half-to-one-pack-a-day smoker.

5. The current cigarette smoker than for the smoker who stopped twenty years ago.

Surgeon General's Conclusions. "Cigarette smoking is the most important cause of chronic obstructive broncho-pulmonary disease in the United States. . . . Ex-cigarette smokers have lower death rates from COBD than do continuing smokers. The cessation of cigarette smoking is associated with improvement in ventilatory function."

APPENDIX E:

Smoking and Other Conditions and Effects

I smoke like a furnace.

W. S. Gilbert
Trial by Jury (1875)

Cigarette smoking by pregnant women has deleterious effects on their unborn fetuses, on birth mortality and birth weight, and is related to death of their children in infancy and to the slower growth and development of those who survive.

Cigarette smokers also suffer certain other diseases, and smoking causes a substantial portion of building fires and forest fires, and is responsible for much loss of life in these holocausts.

Pregnancy and Children

In one study of 2,000 pregnant women, those who smoked had a 20 percent higher number of stillbirths than did nonsmokers. The babies of 17,000 smoking mothers showed "a significantly higher" mortality, attributed mainly to the fact that more of their babies weighed less than 5½ pounds (premature by weight) at birth. In a study of 100,000 births, babies of smoking mothers averaged 6.1 ounces less than those of nonsmokers. Among 48,000 pregnancies, low birth weight was related more to smoking than any other factor. A British study of 17,400 births showed a doubled risk of congenital heart defects among the babies of women who had smoked during pregnancy.

When a pregnant woman smokes, her oxygen-poor blood circulates through her fetus, and this is "probably injurious to fetal tissue," according to Dr. L. D. Longo. A recent Australian study of 4,922 births showed fewer brain cells in the unborn children of smoking mothers. Seven years after birth, the children of women who had smoked heavily during pregnancy had retarded reading ability and lower ratings in social adjustment than the seven-year-old children of nonsmoking mothers.

Gastric Ulcers and Non-Cancerous Mouth Disease

Men who smoke cigarettes get more stomach ulcers, have a higher death rate from peptic ulcers, respond less to antacid treatment for ulcers than do nonsmokers, and heal more slowly after surgery.

Tobacco smokers have higher rates of periodontal disease, which destroys the gums, and trench mouth, an ulcerative condition of the gums, than do nonsmokers. Heavy smokers are more likely to lose teeth, and heal more slowly after tooth extraction. *Stomatitis nicotina,* a precancerous condition of the mouth found most often in pipe smokers, disappears when smoking stops.

Smoking and Fires

Fires caused by smoking are not, of course, a health problem, but they kill and injure just as surely as smoking-caused diseases. Currently, well above one hundred thousand building fires in the United States each year (in one estimate, as many as 25 percent of all building fires) are attributed by the National Fire Protection Association to the careless use of tobacco and the matches used to light cigarettes, cigars, and pipes (this does not include fires caused by children playing with matches). In 1965 the association estimated that such fires caused about eighteen hundred deaths that year. The total is probably higher today.

The facts in this section come from the following sources:

Smoking and Health. Report of the Advisory Committee to the Surgeon General of the Public Health Service. U.S. Department of Health, Education and Welfare. Public Health Service Publication No. 1103. 1964.

The Health Consequences of Smoking. A Public Health Service Review: 1967 U.S. Department of Health, Education and Welfare. Public Health Service Publication No. 1696. 1968.

The Health Consequences of Smoking. 1968 Supplement to the 1967 Public Health Service Review. U.S. Department of Service Publication No. 1696. 1969.

The Health Consequences of Smoking. U.S. Department of Health, Education and Welfare. 1969 Supplement to Public Health Service Publication No. 1969-2. 1970.

The Health Consequences of Smoking. A report of the Surgeon General: 1971 U.S. Department of Health, Education and Welfare. Public Health Service. DHEW Publication No. (HSM) 71–7513.

The Health Consequences of Smoking. A report of the Surgeon General: 1972 U.S. Department of Health, Education and Welfare. Public Health Service. DHEW Publication No. (HSM) 72–7516.

The Health Consequences of Smoking. U.S. Department of Health, Education and Welfare. Public Health Service. DHEW Publication No. (HSM) 73–8704.

Tobacco and Your Health by Harold S. Diehl, M.A., M.D., Sc.D., Special Consultant for Research and Medical Affairs, American Cancer Society, Inc., McGraw-Hill Book Company, New York, 1969. 210 pp. including index plus xi pages of introduction.

Smoking and Health Now. A new report and summary on "Smoking and Its Effects on Health" from the Royal College of Physicians of London—Pitman Medical and Scientific Publishing Co. Ltd., London, England 1971.

ACKNOWLEDGMENTS

This book is based on the thought, experiments, and experiences of a great many people, a number of whom have helped me in researching articles in this field during the past decade. Dr. Daniel Horn of the National Clearinghouse for Smoking and Health has been a pioneer in smoking-cessation research. I have drawn heavily on his advice and work. The self-tests are his, based on the original theories of Dr. Silvan Tomkins. Others at the National Clearinghouse with whom I have worked over the years, and who have always been most helpful, courteous, and considerate are Robert Hutchings and Emil Corwin, two loyal and dedicated public servants; I have also profited from the careful research in medical literature by the various physicians who spent two years at the Clearinghouse, particularly Dr. Elvin Adams and Dr. John Holbrook, both of whom gave me much guidance in the pharmacology of tobacco smoke.

Dr. Donald T. Fredrickson, Project Director, Inter-Society Commission for Heart Disease Resources in New York, has been most generous in making available his creative thinking and wide experience in devising strategies and tactics to help smokers give up cigarettes. Much of the basic thinking in key chapters orginated with Dr. Fredrickson. He has permitted me to borrow from his paper on heart disease before the American Medical Association and on his excellent article "Cigarette Smoking: Questions Patients Ask Doctors," which appeared in *Chest*, vol. 58, 1970, and is the basis for Day Eleven, Section 5, as well as of six case histories in Day Thirteen.

I am also indebted to the American Cancer Society, Inc., for support and cooperation over the past twelve years. The epidemiological work of the society's statistical research department, headed by Dr. E. Cuyler Hammond and Lawrence Garfinkel and their associates, is seminal in the smoking and health fields. Their ongoing Cancer Prevention Study of more than one million American adults is the source for an enormous amount of information. And their various autopsy–epidemiological studies done in conjunction with Dr. Oscar Auerbach of the Veterans Administration have also provided much enlightenment in the physiology and pathology of smoking. I have learned a great deal about smoking cessation in groups from the work of George M. Saunders and Gail Rider of the California division of the society, who based their methods on those of Dr. Fredrickson.

Acknowledgment is hereby made, too, to the Smoking and Health Program of the Canadian Department of National Health and Welfare in Ottawa for permission to borrow case history material from their excellent book *How We Quit Smoking,* in Day Thirteen.

Dr. Sessue I. Hayakawa, former president of San Francisco State College, generously allowed me to quote extensively from his column of June 3–4, 1972, on how he quit smoking, with permission of the Register & Tribune Syndicate, Inc.

A good deal of the reporting on smoking and health has been done by *Reader's Digest* magazine. The editors have been extremely kind in making available materials from various articles I originally researched and wrote for the magazine: "The High Cost of Smoking" (March 1972), "Do You Know What Happens When You Smoke?" (July 1972), "The Truth About Those 'Little Cigars'" (May 1973), and "Better Ways to Stop Smoking" (June 1973).

The manuscript was typed speedily and accurately, as always, by Miss Louise Fisher, who also contributed her personal experience with smoking cessation in Day Thirteen, "I Did It My Way."

WALTER S. ROSS is an author, editor and journalist who has written articles for numerous major magazines. He has written on smoking and health for the past fifteen years for *Reader's Digest* and the American Cancer Society. Mr. Ross is the author of six books, among them *The Last Hero*, a biography of Charles A. Lindbergh.